Praise for Living For Job Seekers

MW01222766

"A fulfilling job in a satisfying career is what most of us seek within our lives. *Living The Dream* offers a unique approach to career and employment search. Anyone in the creative arts knows that it takes more than a well-constructed résumé and a fine portfolio—or list of media credits—to snag work that keeps the juices flowing and life worth living. This book reveals a secret worth sharing: a fulfilling life, one that inspires passion to be and do all that you can, can only be found if you involve everything that makes you human."

> Douglas Spotted Eagle
> Recording Artist/Producer

"This book takes the reader through the same coaching process that I followed with Melanie during my last job search. Melanie's unique approach, which integrates the spiritual, high thought process with the nuts-and-bolts practical details required in any job search, resulted in my finding a position that has been the most satisfying and enjoyable of my entire career."

> Dave Legge
> Chief Financial Officer, Tehama

"Melanie Mulhall has written a comprehensive, caring, and holistic guide to job searching. If you want the book that combines shamanic wisdom with résumé writing strategies, this is it!"

> Tama Kieves
> Author of *This Time I Dance! Trusting*
> *the Journey of Creating the Work You Love*

"Melanie Mulhall has embarked on an interesting journey, one that merges two separate paths and two separate ways of perceiving. She unifies the deeper, mythological path of the shaman, who pays attention to intuitive streams of knowledge, with the more external path through ordinary reality, where we concentrate on linear progress and concrete, logical results. It is high time for our inner and outer realities to merge and for that synthesis to take on greater creditability. Finding the intuitive in business or in the process of living a mundane life always brings greater success and expanded enjoyment. So drop into the new perception Melanie offers here, and enjoy your own discoveries!"

Penney Peirce
Author of *The Intuitive Way, The Present Moment, and Dreams for Dummies*

"An intriguing adventure into the heretofore-dark passage of job search and career development. Finally, a map that utilizes the totality of the individual as a unique entity."

Antonio Arguello
Shaman, author of *The Death of the Last Dragon*

"*Living The Dream* is a remarkable book, and especially for those whose job search and thoughts of career shift emerge from a fundamental dissatisfaction with their work history. It combines the most practical, marketable advice for finding *your right path* with a psychological, philosophical, holistic, spiritual and humanistic understanding of the way the world (the universe) works. *Practical and do-able transformation* in your own world of work (and life and relationships) is what this book offers. Who can refuse that invitation?"

Warren Ziegler
Author of *When Your Spirit Calls–In Search of Your Spiritual Archetype* and *Ways of Enspiriting: Transformative Practices for the Twenty-First Century*

May you live a beautiful dream! Melanie Mulhall

Living The Dream

A Guidebook For Job Seekers And Career Explorers

Melanie Mulhall

Dragonheart Publishing, LLC
Broomfield, Colorado

in conjunction with

Dragon Ink Publications
Lakewood, Colorado

The instructions and advice in this book are not intended as a substitute for legal advice, psychological counseling, or medical advice. The author and publishers disclaim any responsibility or liability resulting from actions advocated or discussed in this book. Those desiring or needing legal advice medical advice, and/or counseling are encouraged to seek the services of competent professionals in those areas of expertise.

The compact disc accompanying this book should not be played while driving, operating equipment, or otherwise engaged in activity that could prove hazardous when done conjointly with listening to and experiencing its content. The author and publishers disclaim any responsibility or liability resulting from ignoring this caution.

Published by:

Dragonheart Publishing, LLC
1093 E. 3rd Ave.
Broomfield, CO 80020

in conjunction with

Dragon Ink Publications
3120 Xenon St.
Lakewood, CO 80215

Living The Dream–A Guidebook For Job Seekers And Career Explorers
Copyright © 2002 by Melanie Mulhall
All rights reserved. This book and CD, or parts thereof, may not be used or reproduced in any form without the permission of Dragonheart Publishing, LLC

Printed in the United States of America

First Edition

Library of Congress Control Number: 2002093644
ISBN 0-9723295-0-1

Book/Cover design by Nick Zelinger, NZ Graphics
Cover Art by Isaac Hartsell
Author photograph by Howard Cornell

Contents

INVOCATION

Statistics say there are more than six billion human beings on our planet Earth, our Mother Earth. In all the billions of people, there is only one of *You*. You are the Creator of your own reality. You are the only person on this planet who can choose how you want to see life, live life, dance life, walk life, feel life and relate to all of life.

Create the most loving, trusting, and compassionate life for yourself, for when you create this life for yourself, you will know peace, love, and compassion. Your life will be in balance and understanding will be your scepter. When we understand, we have no expectations, no judgments, and no fear of life.

Give what you can, take only what you need, smile, and look at life through the Creator's Eyes.

Marilyn Youngbird
Bailey, Colorado
July, 2002

ACKNOWLEDGEMENTS

The creation of this book was a journey. I was joined on the road by many pilgrims who made the trip easier for me than it would have otherwise been. I am grateful for their willingness to make a part of the journey with me and for lending me their support when the road became weary.

Thank you, Kacy Brown and Tricia Sargent, for your brilliant editing. The book–and my writing–are the better for it. Thank you, Warren Ziegler, for your review of the book in its nascence and thank you for teaching me to listen to the voice of my own spirit. Thank you also to Antonio Arguello, Terry Gleason, Cindy Landis-Combes, Erika Niemann, Helena Mariposa, and Lisa Niederman for your review and proofing of the work as it neared completion. You saved me from a few embarrassments and carried me through the tediousness of the final editing and proofing.

Don Antonio Arguello, your patience, wisdom, and kinship have facilitated my ongoing transformation. Without you, this book might never have been finished. Without you, I would not be the spiritual warrior I am today. No day passes without my gratitude for you, sensei.

Thank you, Marilyn Youngbird, for your love and guidance. Thank you, also, for the sweat lodges that helped manifest this work and for bringing me to the grandmothers and grandfathers in a beautiful way.

Thank you Cindy, Carol, Douglas, Gary, Howard, John, Kacy, Larry, Melissa...and all the rest...for the stories that have enriched this book and will help to illuminate the paths of its readers.

Thank you, Douglas Spotted Eagle, for taking my concept of a CD to accompany the book and making it a reality. At a time when I was overwhelmed with the task, you came in and took on the project with elegance, grace, and impeccability. You are proof that there are angels among us. Thank you, also, for the inspiration of your music and your friendship, the energy of which have been woven into the fabric of this book.

Thank you, Ron Grandia, for bringing the guided imageries to life. Your editorial suggestions helped the guided imageries become the lyrical magic I always intended for them. You are their voice–and mine. You are also my alter-ego little brother, something that gives me great pleasure.

Thank you, Nick Zelinger, for your ability to read the energy I brought to this project and for your skill in translating it into form. Thank you also for the music and lyrics that not only reminded me who I was, but which you have so graciously allowed to be reprinted.

Thank you, Isaac Hartsell, for your creativity, patience, willingness, and good spirit in creating the art work for the book. I needed to hear an enthusiastic "Yes!" from the Universe and you were that *yes*.

Thank you, Sally McDonald, for your persistent and loving encouragement. You saw that I was a writer. I knew it, at some level, but it was your encouragement that helped me step into it.

Thank you, Cindy Landis-Combes, for being the dear, dear friend that you are and for being my most enthusiastic cheerleader. Your belief in me helped me maintain my belief in myself.

Thank you, Lisa Niederman, for being a kindred spirit and for your support as I repaired certain parts of my energetic blueprint and began to imprint what I needed onto that field.

A heartfelt thank you to all of my clients–current, past, and future–for teaching me as much as I have taught you, for inspiring me on a regular basis, and for helping to keep me humble.

Thank you, dear peers and fellow members of the Colorado Independent Publishers Association for demonstrating in hundreds of ways that I could do it myself without doing it alone.

Thank you, Howard Cornell. As both husband and friend, you have added texture and quality to my life. As writer extraordinaire, you have managed to maintain the delicate balance between support and distance while I grew into my own voice. As the extraordinary human being you are, you have maintained incredible equanimity during the roller coaster ride of my transformation.

Sometimes there are people in our lives who have major impact on who we are and how we move through life without ever knowing that they have done so. Many people have had this kind of impact on my life, and I would like to acknowledge two of them here. Marianne Williamson, thank you for your earthiness, your wisdom, your caring for all humankind, and your many teachings. Your help was invaluable during my own career explorations and job searches. Thank you, also, to Oprah Winfrey. Oprah, you have made *spirit* a word that could be uttered joyfully and openly by daring to do so yourself. You are a beautiful model of honesty and authenticity. You have motivated me and moved my heart over the course of many years, and I thank you for that.

Finally, my loyalty, gratitude and thanks to the guidance that has lifted me, exalted me, humbled me and been my army of personal coaches. You have provided many lessons in a sweet and gentle way and a few with a sledgehammer. Thank you for both. I need not name you, but you, my council and my ambassadors, have played a role that, like the journey, cannot be described and will not be denied.

INTRODUCTION

> *"...every ebb and flow reminds me of the journey*
> *that cannot be described and will not be denied."*
> Nick Zelinger, *This Fragile Body*

*M*y clients have suggested that I alert my readers to the fact that this is not the typical book on job search or career. Consider this fair warning. This book's approach to career and job search is a holistic one. Rather than compartmentalizing your life, the philosophy expressed in this book is one that celebrates your being as a composite of mind, body, spirit, and emotions. Life is a journey and while your career is an exciting aspect of that journey, it must be embraced within the larger journey, not considered an isolated aspect of it.

The approach to career exploration and job search presented here is richly infused with my own life experience and training in career/life/executive coaching, corporate consulting, human resources, energy work,[1] and shamanism.[2] That experience and training have led me to the following conclusions: **We are all dreaming our lives and we are all living that dream. Whether the dream is a beautiful one or a nightmare is the choice each of us makes. Given that you are already living the dream, you might as well play an active role in it!**

To re-examine a career or job search from only an intellectual and physical perspective is to impoverish the process. There *are* components to this process that should be approached with your rational/logical capabilities and you *do* need to take action in the physical world. **But if you are to live your**

dreams, you must allow your dreams to live *you* every bit as much as you live *them*. For this, you need to function more holistically than the recipe books on career and job search typically suggest.

The approach presented here as holistic is an approach that acknowledges Universal Principles.[3] That is, it bows to the accumulated understanding over millennia of human experience, both that experience blessed with Divine inspiration and that blessed with the inspiration derived from the mental and physical sweat of humankind. This is not so much a new approach when applied to career and job search as it is an approach that has languished through years of business community pretense that the human spirit can somehow be disembodied, leaving a thinking/doing human devoid of feeling and spiritual qualities.

Anyone lacking passion for his or her current career or job understands, at a deep level, that the disembodied approach does not work well for those wanting more than a paycheck for work that engages body and mind without engaging spirit and emotions. Likewise, anyone engaging in career exploration or job search who wants more than money for time understands that while the body and mind can be bought, the spirit and emotions do not, necessarily, come along for the ride if they are not welcomed into the process and if their needs are not taken into consideration.

This book examines career exploration and job search as a journey that, in acknowledging Universal Principles, brings the fourfold nature of the human being (mind, body, spirit and emotions) to bear on the process of discerning and finding right work. Right work, in this book's vernacular, means work that either feeds all parts of that fourfold nature or work that brings one closer to feeding that fourfold nature.

Throughout this book, you will find career exploration and job search likened to a grand journey. This comparison was not undertaken casually. *Life* is a journey and the process of discerning and discovering right work is a part of that journey. With this understanding, enter into the dream of the heroic journey. The heroic journey is an archetypal representation of the process of life, applicable whether one is actually a budding *hero* or *heroine.* It involves:

- Disengaging from the assumption that culturally accepted models are correct,
- Traveling (inwardly, outwardly, or both) towards a discovery of what is true to one's Self,
- Overcoming obstacles along the way,
- Discovering and claiming one's power, and
- Returning (whether one has physically left or not) to claim a life that is richer and fuller because of that discovery, serving the world in the process.

This is exactly the process possible to those in job search or career exploration!

While this book does not attempt a mythological or archetypal comparison to the career exploration/job search process and the heroic journey, understand that if you have been drawn to this book because you are in job search or are exploring your career, it *is* possible for you to accomplish more than finding a job or re-evaluating your career. You may engage in a process that:

- Encourages you to disengage from the culturally accepted model of career as usual, devoid of spirit,
- Encourages you to travel both inwardly and outwardly towards an acknowledgement of yourself as a four-fold human being, one with body, mind, spirit and emotions,
- Assists you in overcoming the obstacles along the way,
- Encourages and assists you in discovering your true Self and reclaiming your power, and
- Helps you discover what is right work for you and live a life that is richer and fuller than the life you have allowed yourself to live thus far.

I have come to this approach through more than an intellectual process. I have intimate experience with it. My own career has spanned government service, the not-for-profit sector, and corporate America.

After twenty years in the field of human resources, I dropped out and became apprenticed to a shaman. What happened next was a period of accelerated learning and testing.

When I began that apprenticeship, I still held the belief, in some part of my being, that I would re-enter corporate life. There was plenty of information to the contrary, both internal and external. At a deep level, my larger self understood the truth before my head and heart accepted it. I immersed myself in the apprenticeship. It was a 24/7 operation. I "did the work" on myself. I found myself spontaneously recapitulating my life. The visions and sixth-sense experiences I had occasionally experienced became daily occurrences. I burned through that apprenticeship quickly, though it was not without cost. I experienced a dark night of the soul and found myself even more confused about my life path. My husband wondered what had happened to me and when the apprenticeship and the chaos it created in our simple life would be over.

In the process of that apprenticeship, I changed, quite literally, down to the level of the DNA, down to the bones, as a shaman might put it. I was no longer the woman I had been in the corporate arena, yet I was more fully myself than I had ever been in my life. I stepped into my destiny and found my life's work in the process.

I had experience with career/executive/life coaching, but what I had been offering people became real at more than an intellectual or even emotional level. It became real in a visceral sense. I began to take more risks in the career coaching work, to present some things in the terms I understood—as Universal Principles. I had been concerned about doing this. Would people think I was too *out there?* Would I alienate potential clients? Would anything I had to say make sense?

I found, to my surprise and delight, that people were far more open to Universal Principles than I had suspected. Some clients even seemed to breathe a sigh of relief that their whole lives were being taken into consideration, not just their work lives, and that the previously unspoken mystery of things was being addressed.

As in the mastery of any sport or spiritual practice, the process of career coaching from the perspective of Universal Principles is an ongoing honing, refining and developing of capacity and expression. This book is not an end in itself, but represents some of the insights and illumination I have found along the path. As in any walk in the wilderness, every turn in the path, every new vista, every clearing in a densely wooded area brings amazing sights and sounds. Here a Stellar's jay, there a wild iris, on a nearby hill a mule deer, across the path a stream and ahead, the mysterious. The path continues.

Entering Into The Journey

If you have found your way to *this* book, then you are probably aware that there are dozens of books addressing career exploration and job search. Many of those books have created a well-worn path and one that I have no interest in treading. I ask you to go off that path for a time. I ask you to hike through a wilderness that may seem both mysterious and eerily familiar to many of you; mysterious because you may never have approached career exploration or job search in quite this way; familiar because you may have brought this approach to other parts of your life.

There is no denying that the re-evaluation of one's career entails reason, planning, hard work, and perseverance. But I have found that enthusiasm for the journey cannot be found in the intellect, but in that part of us where passion and creativity reside: the part that gets so involved in process that you forget about outcome; that loves the journey as much or more than the destination; that loves inquiry more than answers; that senses and intuits as much as it thinks. Enthusiasm for the search, in other words, resides in your soul life.

Because of this, you may find that this book affects you more viscerally than intellectually. Think back to a time in your life when major change, viewed by you as positive, happened within and to you. Your friends, family, and acquaintances may have viewed this change as surprising, shocking, or out of character. The change may have seemed so to you, too.

But thinking back, you know that the seeds for this change were planted internally long before they gave blossom externally. They lived for a time in the rich compost of your inner being. They expressed themselves viscerally before expressing themselves in external action.

Let the message of this book seep into you. Think about it, but feel it more. Let it seep into the subconscious. What is meaningful to you and what is useful will rise to consciousness and manifest externally. You may find that some part of you is drawn to a new avenue of soulful experience and expression.

This book explores the soulful side of career planning and job search, the mystery of it, the aspects that resonate with the internal life's own ongoing search for more than a job. It beckons you to get off the rational, linear path just long enough to discover your own stirrings within and to find the path with spirit.

This book is *not* about religion. Churches, cathedrals, monasteries, and ashrams abound for those who want to explore religion. It *is* about the spiritual path, the personal spiritual path, apart from dogma or doctrine. It invites you to de-compartmentalize your life enough to give your career exploration and/or job search the room for the soul's instruction to it.

May your journey be a soulful one and may you live your dream!

Chapter 1

THE JOURNEY BEGINS

It is the quality of your combined being and doing
that will determine where the journey takes you.

Perhaps you are beginning a job search. You have left an organization or are still employed by one but have decided it is time to move on. You may not be able to see it now and you may not believe it if anyone else tells you, but you have a marvelous opportunity for this to be a great adventure and a time of riveting introspection. Your journey may take you not only to your next creative engagement in the form of a job, but also home to yourself.

You may find yourself seeing with great clarity, listening to your own internal voice and hearing with resonance the words of others, feeling strange and powerful internal stirrings, smelling the roses or your beloved's skin with heightened pleasure, tasting life fully, and being stirred by your own mental rumblings and ruminations in a way that is more profound than ever before. Or you may not. The difference lies in how you equip yourself for the journey and how your feet find their footfalls. While you are *doing*, that is, making the journey itself, you may also find yourself *being* with a new depth. It is the quality of your combined being and doing that will determine where the journey takes you.

Let us suppose that foreign travel is one of the great joys of your life. You have never been to Provence and you yearn to travel in that sunny and redolent part of France. You get brochures. You talk with friends who have made that journey. You speak with a travel agent. Your French is rusty so you buy books and tapes to help you relearn the language, knowing that the Provencal dialect and vocabulary is slightly different than the Parisian French represented on those books and tapes. You also buy travel books, some that are mostly photographic representations of this beautiful region and some that tell of its history, culture, annual events and the must-see sights.

You begin to gather equipment and attire for the journey. Your attire will depend on the time of year and you will want to account for all the conditions you may encounter, so you bring casual clothing for warm weather, rain gear, sweaters and jackets you can layer, swim wear for your time along the Côte d'Azur, sturdy walking shoes, a hat to protect you from the sun and, finally, ensembles that will make you feel at ease in the finest restaurants.

You gather together your alarm clock, a few good books for airplane and quiet moment reading, a flashlight, and all the other accouterments you either need or that will make you feel at home in your own skin, even though you will be on foreign soil. Your passport is up to date and you have checked into the issue of visas.

You begin to visualize the journey as you plot out where you will be and when you will be there. You know there will be considerable walking on the trip you are planning for yourself, so you get yourself in good physical shape for the journey. You know the trip will entail both planned and unplanned expense, and you have saved for this travel, but you now begin to set aside some of your usual luxuries to ensure that you can be worry free about the expense of the journey itself. You have always traveled by yourself, but this time you decide to join a group, so you make arrangements with a tour company.

The entire time you plan for this trip, you clarify for yourself what you want out of it. You have read everything that Peter Mayle has written about Provence and you want to see it for yourself. You want to learn something about Provencal people and Provencal life. You look forward to good food and the good company of your travel group, but you also build in time for quiet reflection and leisurely solitude. You decide that whatever happens, you are going to enjoy this trip. Weather conditions, changes in plans, *nothing* will keep you from having a good time. You bring this mindset to the trip in part because you are a fundamentally positive person, but also because you are an experienced traveler and know that this mindset makes all the difference in the quality of the trip.

Departure day arrives. You arise early, drive to the airport and park your car in long-term parking. You are excited, but then, airports always excite you. You check your luggage, find your terminal, make it through security, have a cup of coffee and, after a short wait, board your plane. You fly from Denver to Boston, where other members of the tour join you. From Boston, the flight will take you directly to Nice.

In Boston, you meet a somewhat curmudgeonly middle-aged man and his patient wife, both of whom are in your tour group. The man is distressed because he has met some other tour members, four young women who are loud and who chain-smoke cigarettes. Agitated, he states that he cannot stand to be around cigarette smoke and implies, rather vaguely, that he needs to avoid it because of his health. He obsesses about this right up to the time that you board your airplane. You are grateful that you are not seated close to him.

When you finally arrive at the Nice airport, after many changes in time zone and the experience of watching day turn to night and night turn back into day, you are a bit stiff and quite tired. You have slept little during the flight. You breeze through customs and meet your tour guide. He is an enthusiastic young man and you begin to get something of a second wind as you wait for the remainder of the tour group to assemble. The air is balmy and tropical plants abound. Your curmudgeonly acquaintance? He grumbles, he sighs, and he seems to be oblivious to the beauty around him.

Your journey proves to be better than you imagined. You travel that first day to La Palud-sur-Verdon. On the way, your tour stops at a charming café and you have your first taste of pastis, that rich liqueur favored by the Provencals. The next day is a bit misty, so your group is unable to walk down into the Grand Canyon du Verdon, but you are not discouraged. You are able to stop at many viewing points to see the canyon and it is breathtaking.

Over the next two weeks, you visit Moustiers-Ste-Marie, Riez, Greoux-les-Bains, Manosque, Aix-en-Provence, Marseilles, Cassis, Arles, Avignon, St-Remy-de-Provence, Les-Baux-de-Provence and Nice. You eat bread so crispy on the outside and soft on the inside it nearly brings tears to your eyes. You become addicted to tapenade and find the regional cheese to be the best you have ever tasted. You discover that you adore truffles, savor tarts of many varieties, and otherwise lose yourself in gas-tronomical heaven. You drink French press coffee in the morning and wine with both midday and evening meals. The wine, even the inexpen-sive wine, is good. You have no trouble with your weight because you walk with vigor for long periods every day.

You see ancient Roman ruins that inspire you to reflect on the mean-ing of your own life within the context of millennia. You not only visit places painted by Gaugin and Cezanne, but you visit museums that house some of their original artwork and you visit both Cezanne's studio and the asylum at which Van Gogh stayed for a time after slicing off part of his ear. You visit the open-air markets and participate with the group in mak-ing a meal, under the tutelage of a French chef, after purchasing the meal's ingredients very early that morning at the market in Manosque. You hike within view of Mt. Ste Victoire, see the *calanques* from high above them, walk hundreds of steps up to the shrine overlooking the city of Moustiers-Ste-Marie, walk through the Luberon and otherwise test the physical endurance you have been building in preparation for this trip. You taste wine and olive oil in the wine cellar of a castle, see the wild horses of the Camargue, visit the Palace of the Popes in Avignon and ride a barge down the Rhone.

Of course, you do miss some sites. There are also some changes in plan, mostly to accommodate an occasional rainy day. Most of the hotels you stay in are lovely, but all are not as nice as the best of them. The travel brochures talked of picnics to punctuate the long walks you would take on this trip, but the picnics really constitute brown bag lunches eaten sitting on a log. You take everything in stride, discovering that you enjoy what you see and do when the schedule changes as much as when you stay on schedule. The people are friendly and kind to you as you practice your clumsy French on them. The weather is, at best, idyllic. At worst, the weather is a perfectly acceptable change from idyllic. You are thankful that there is no mistral during your visit!

What about the curmudgeon? He complains about the smokers throughout the trip, even though they scrupulously do their smoking downwind of him and at distance. The hotel beds are too soft. The food is too rich. There is either too much or not enough walking on any given day and it is always at the wrong pace. He does not find the people friendly, but makes no attempt to speak in French. He has read so much about Provence and has seen so many travelogues that the sites seem almost anticlimactic to him. He resents even one hour of rain. He is easily bored. Changes in plan seem to disrupt him internally.

You and the curmudgeon take the same trip, but the two of you do not have the same journey. Fortunately, you do not allow the curmudgeon to affect the quality of your trip.

It is really up to you. You live in an abundant Universe. You can choose to believe in its abundance and benevolence, thereby tapping into it, or you can feel deprived. This will not be simply in your head, but in your experience. While it is true that you are served by being happy with what you now have instead of waiting for something to make you happy, that is not what I refer to when suggesting that you can choose to believe in abundance. As humans on planet Earth, there is love and there is fear. That is pretty much it. The Universe fully supports you when you choose love because love is the ultimate substance of which the greater Universe is made. When you choose love, you are choosing to experience oneness with the Universe. When you choose fear, you are choosing separation from it. Choose whatever you like, but I recommend choosing love. To do so is to make a very practical choice because in doing so you honor your own Spirit and create a Divine partnership for the journey.

Let The Journey Begin

I have proposed that whenever you begin to examine your career path, whether it is a matter of simply taking a fresh look or beginning an all-out job search, it can be thought of as a journey. It is true that the journey may have a destination, but the journey itself, and the way you make it, affects the outcome. So, let the journey begin!

Life offers many journeys and many ways to make the journey. Throughout this book, I will offer vignettes, stories to shift your thinking and/or illuminate the path as you journey. Many of these vignettes are the real stories of clients, some are composites, some come from my own life experience, and some were created to make a point. While most of the stories refer to career and job search, not all do. The story of every human's life is written from rich and varied experiences. Each experience is related to the whole of that person's life, not merely to a part of it. Realize, then, that all of the vignettes offer something to illuminate the path of your career exploration/job search journey.

These first two vignettes, stories from the shamanic tradition, suggest that there are inner and outer forms of journey. This is a concept with which you will become more familiar as we continue. As you read these stories, understand that they are metaphors for the career exploration/job search journey, providing inner and outer roadmaps for that journey.

An Otherworld Journey

The shaman She Who Keeps Fire Alive prepares for a journey. This is a journey to and within an alternative reality, an altered state of conscious-

---

ness. While she has journeyed many times on her own, this is a special journey. Because of this, she has requested the help of another shaman, the shaman to whom she was once apprenticed, the shaman named Awakens Many Spirits.

She has asked Awakens Many Spirits to facilitate her journey. He will guide her, as she lies upon his animal skin rug, through a state of progressive relaxation. He will smudge her and the room in which she departs on her journey. He will drum for her. And he will hold the space for her, that is, add his intent to her own, enter a meditative state, support her as she transcends time and space, and provide energetic protection for her while she journeys.

Keeps Fire Alive, as she is commonly known, spends several days preparing for this journey. She purifies herself by fasting, entering a time of complete silence, meditating and performing several rounds of sweats in a nearby thermal pool. She sets her intent. She allows herself to walk between the worlds during this time of preparation, to open herself to the guidance of her spirit guides, power animals and the Great Spirit that lives in all things.

On the day of the journey, she picks flowers from her garden, being careful to offer a prayer and a sprinkling of corn meal for their sacrifice. She also selects a candle for the altar in the journey room and a piece of fruit, as offering to the spirit realm. Her intent is fixed as she rubs her body with salt while bathing. She allows her intuition to guide her to appropriate accoutrements for the journey. Before she leaves for the home of Awakens Many Spirits, she dons her bear fetish necklace. She is ready for the journey, wherever it will take her.

A Journey Across Mother Earth

The shaman, She Who Keeps Fire Alive, plans a journey to a remote part of the world. For many years, she has contemplated this journey and now finds that circumstances have conspired to manifest it. The funding she has needed to make the journey has materialized, rather magically. She seeks the counsel of a friend who has traveled to this part of the world, meets with him and listens to many stories of his experiences there. She asks questions and is given advice about the journey. All of this is useful information and she feels blessed to have a friend who has traveled this path before and can help make her way easier.

She prepares in other ways for the trip as well. She sets her intent and plans her itinerary while, at the same time, planning for the unexpected. She eats well, meditates, gets sufficient sleep and exercises her body. She takes care of what must be taken care of in her daily life so she may leave the country without concern about what might happen in her absence. Finally, she opens herself to whatever the Universe offers in the way of signs and guidance in the form of dreams and visions, synchronicities, the presence and activities of birds and other animals, changes in weather patterns and everything else that presents itself around her. When the day comes for her departure, she feels alive and ready for the experience, whatever it will be.

Chapter 2

EQUIPPING YOURSELF FOR THE TRIP: WHAT TO TAKE AND WHAT TO LEAVE BEHIND

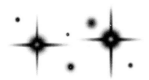

...you cannot get to where you are going if you do not know where you are or if you refuse to take a step forward.

*Y*our journey will be more comfortable, pleasant and profitable if you give attention to your preparation for it. While preparation for career exploration/job search is different in form than preparation for a trip to Provence or some other geographic destination, your life's journey does have its own geography to be considered, and carefully equipping yourself for the next part of that journey is no less important than equipping yourself for a trip abroad. Consider the following:

- Prepare by accepting where you are today, by accepting things as they are.
- Prepare by getting yourself a guide for the journey, in the form of a coach.
- Prepare by doing some R & R.
- Prepare by unburdening yourself from the past, by "clearing" organizations and people for whom you feel an emotional charge.
- Prepare by accepting yourself and who you are.
- Prepare by working with your "shadow side" as you develop deeper levels of self-acceptance.
- Prepare by doing your homework.

Accepting Things As They Are

Every journey you take in your life, including the career journey, begins exactly where you are at the moment. Where you are at the moment is your launching pad. While you can fantasize about getting to Provence from London, if you are actually in Pittsburgh at the moment, you will only delay *getting* to Provence by thinking of yourself as being somewhere other than Pittsburgh. The route from Pittsburgh to Provence is different than the route from London to Provence.

You may have recently left an organization, believe that you need to make a change as part of a strategic career plan, or just feel the romance is gone with your current work and hear an internal voice saying it is time to move on. You may have once viewed that organization as a haven, a place where you would long reside. Alternatively, you may have viewed your employment there as a relationship of creative engagement that would continue as long as the potential for you to work creatively and be fairly rewarded for it was there. You probably have forged friendships at the organization. You probably have extended yourself through long hours and hard work, proud of your contribution and proud to be connected with its products or services. However you have related to the organization, its people, its products and/or services, if you have already left the organization or seriously intend to do so, it is important to begin the process of intellectual and emotional separation.

Images and feelings of divorce or the death of a loved one may come to you in waves as you contemplate separation from the organization. Or you may feel great relief, as if you are ridding yourself of something toxic in your life. Whatever the sensation, it is likely to be powerful. This is not surprising since most of us put a great deal of ourselves into our work, not simply in the long hours we work, but in the physical, mental, emotional and spiritual energy we give to it. Leaving an organization is never trivial, whether you have been a part of it for ten months or ten years. Honor the significance to your life of your departure from the organization. Then accept it. In the simplest of terms, you cannot get to where you are going if you do not know where you are or if you refuse to take a step forward.

So, accept things as they are, accept that your relationship with the organization is at or may be nearing its end. If you have been involuntarily separated and have feelings of anger, allow them to pass through you but not settle into you. Anger will not serve you for long. Do the same with feelings of remorse, fear, and sentimentality.

One of the saddest things I have witnessed in my career, and I have witnessed it many times, is the person who, having left an organization, persists in clinging to it. Some people spend months blaming everything and everyone for the demise of the relationship. Others insist on finishing off every piece of work before they leave and staying in almost constant touch with the organization's activities and people after they leave. Both are fear-based reactions, both stifle the creative energy needed to move forward, and both deny the basic truth that the chapter in your life about your time with that organization has been fully written. Choose again, turn the page, free up the energy of forward motion, and accept that the journey begins now with this step.

A Guide For The Journey

The right guide can make all the difference in the journey. Whether you are going to a familiar place or traveling in uncharted territory, a guide can point out what you might otherwise miss and help keep you on track. If outplacement services are being provided by or being negotiated with an organization you are leaving, do everything you can to gain and exercise the right to select an outplacement coach suited to you and your needs. Not everyone has a network that includes professionals in the outplacement industry and you may be unaware of the differing services provided by different providers. Your organization may have created a career center service because of a reduction in force (downsizing, rightsizing, or however else they term it). They may have an exclusive contract for services by a given provider or they may simply believe they can select the best coach for you. What serves you, however, is maximum flexibility in the selection of providers and services.

What do you need? Are you equipped with a home office and feel both comfortable and productive there or do you need office space outside your home? Do you need clerical help? Does spending time in group meetings with others in job search seem like fruitful behavior to you or more like a waste of time? Do you need serious help in refining your résumé or do you simply need someone with knowledge about résumés to review it and provide input? Does your search require expert strategizing? Do you need gentle pushing? The answers to these questions relate to the level and type of outplacement services you will need.

But perhaps most important is the chemistry between you and your coach. Because it is so important, you need a say in it. Do not simply accept someone assigned to you and do not think that the person who was a great coach for someone else will, necessarily, be a great coach for you. You need to talk to, meet with, and even interview the people you or your organization are considering for the role of coach.

There are many providers of outplacement services these days, including large national organizations and small local boutique firms. Some provide service by the book, and it is a cookbook. They will tell you that there is a tried and true method for conducting job search and your role is to surrender yourself to the method. Do not buy it! Yes, there are some things that, over time, have proven helpful. But today is not yesterday and tomorrow may be light years from today.

Further, you are not everyone else in job search. You are unique with a set of life experiences, talents, passions and needs that are different from those of everyone else. Your uniqueness needs to be honored and the spiritual connection between you and your next opportunity needs to be acknowledged and made an ongoing part of the work with you. Look for chemistry between you and your coach. Look for someone who honors you and the spiritual quest that is your journey.

But what if outplacement services have not been provided or you are exploring your career options while still employed? If you have left an organization and have either negotiated or been provided a relatively rich separation package, fund your own outplacement assistance. If this is not possible, then find yourself a coach among your friends and acquaintances. Notice that I did not include family. Your family will play an important role of support in your search, but should not play the role of coach. Why? Because families are complex systems and no family system provides the objectivity or the engaged but dispassionate attention to your needs that a coach can.

Ideally, the coach you find among your friends will be someone who has been through job search himself within the past five years and is spiritually, though not necessarily religiously, oriented. Your coach needs to be willing to meet with you periodically, preferably in person, at least part of the time. Your coach needs to be willing to serve for the duration of the search, realizing that the frequency of contact will likely be greater early on, and then taper off a bit, to be increased again as needed.

You may wonder why you need a coach at all. You may have had some bad experiences in the past with teachers, advisors, athletic coaches or the little old lady who used to come once a week to give you piano lessons when you were ten. It has been said that the lawyer who attempts to represent herself has a fool for a lawyer and a fool for a client. This is a matter of objectivity and judgment. It is also remarkably similar to the difference between massaging yourself, even if you are a professional massage therapist, and engaging someone else to massage you. My own experience, both as a person in job search/career exploration and as a coach for others, is that the journey is more productive, more fruitful, and more pleasant when you engage a coach.

The role of the coach is that of advisor, mentor, provocateur, catalyst, mirror and spiritual companion. You cannot do these things for yourself. Just as the infusion of energy from outside of yourself into your energy field plays a part in the therapeutic effect of being massaged by another, so do the thinking, spirit and energy of the coach play an important and salubrious role in your search.

A good coach will, among other things:

- Help you get mentally and emotionally "clear" of the organization that you have left or wish to leave;
- Ask you to identify your strengths and weaknesses;
- Have you do some visualizing about your "ideal" job;
- Ask you to articulate your boundaries (geographic, monetary, etc.);
- Help you update your résumé;
- Identify roadblocks to your search and what to do about them;
- Coach you on sourcing potential employers;
- Support you in your spiritual, intellectual, emotional and physical growth efforts;
- Help you prepare for interviews and debrief with you following interviews;
- Work with you to keep your search on track;
- Serve as sounding board and cheering section;
- Help you manage the emotional roller coaster that comes with job search;
- Talk through offers with you;
- Advise you during negotiations; and
- Celebrate with you once you have secured your next position.

In other words, a good coach is an invaluable aid.

Some coaches come equipped with a spiritual bent, but many do not. Do not count on your coach to be your spiritual advisor during your search, but do demand that s/he honor the importance of this aspect of the search.

You may find the guidance provided by other coaches helpful at this time, too. If you have never examined yourself at depth with the aid of a therapist, now may be a good time to do so. The days of viewing therapists as crutches for the mentally disturbed or idle rich are long over. Many therapists work exclusively, or almost exclusively, with ordinary people who are in life transition. Your insurance may cover all or part of this work. Having been on both sides of the therapist's desk, alternately as therapist and therapist's client, I can heartily recommend the process. Just as a good tour guide can point out sights you may have missed or identify flora and fauna that are unfamiliar to you, a good therapist can facilitate your trip.

Likewise, if you are affiliated with a particular religion, you may find the guidance of a religious counselor helpful at this time. Whether or not you subscribe to a particular religion, some work with a trained shaman may also be of benefit to you. I admit to being somewhat prejudiced about the value of shamanic practice. The personal work I did as apprentice to a shaman was instrumental in a personal mental and spiritual detoxification and renewal process. Admittedly, not every city and hamlet has a resident shaman, but more of them are in practice than is commonly known. It is well worth the effort to seek one out, check out his or her reputation, discern whether doing some work together might be of help and, if so, add that person to your coaching team.

R & R

The meaning of R & R changed for me when I left a company at which I had worked for seven years. Instead of Rest & Recreation, R & R came to mean Recovery & Reflection. Do not misunderstand. It was a good company. It had just ceased to be a good company for me. I had worked ten to twelve hour days under conditions of high stress for so long I could no longer invoke the sense of what any other way of working was like. My most prevalent feeling when I left was relief.

As a good human resource professional, I did for myself what any good outplacement organization would counsel a long-term employee to do when she leaves a company: I allowed myself to have feelings about leaving the company. I let it be okay to feel absolute joy about leaving one day and grief the next.

Mostly I forgave myself and I forgave the company. Recovery and reflection are not part of the victim mentality that abounds. They are also not the quick fix many people want. We do not seem to have a very high tolerance in our society for the time it takes to feel our feelings, examine our experience to learn from it, and heal. We want to rush it.

The ruminations of the soul take time. Recovery takes time. If you risk telling friends or family you are feeling emotionally punk or unsettled, you may be encouraged to look at the bright side, count your blessings, and have a stiff upper lip. If your feelings persist for more than a day or two, it may be suggested that you see a doctor, take a Valium or just get over it. If you follow that advice, you may be missing an opportunity to experience yourself more deeply and fully, to experience a depth of darkness out of which a brighter light may emerge. Sometimes there is value in summoning the courage to live with the darkness for a time. It can provide an opportunity to learn something about your self-doubts, your fears, your regrets, and those parts of you that sometimes want to choose rage and revenge, even if you know better. You cannot transform the darkness by denying it or medicating it. You transform it by having the courage to look at it, feel it, and perform a kind of spiritual alchemy on it as you allow it to move through you.

If recovery and reflection are not about rushing it, what *are* they about? They are an initiation. They are a rite of passage. When you allow yourself to become really engaged in the process of recovery and reflection, when you combine it with finding joy in your day-to-day and moment-by-moment experience, there is the power of transformation to it. You know yourself better and you become more authentic. You catch yourself in stress behavior sooner and know what to do about it, before it becomes toxic. You follow where your values lead you. You take responsibility for your own joy.

There are many ways to engage the transformative power of recovery and reflection. It helps to disengage from the interruptions of everyday life through meditation, solitude, time spent in nature, or any other tool that assists you in going within.

One of my personal tools for creating an environment that facilitates reflection and recovery has been spending time at the Carmelite monastery in Crestone, Colorado. At the foot of the Sangre de Cristo Mountains, this monastery happens to house both male and female monks. Each "retreatant" (person doing a week-long retreat) has his or her own hermitage, both beautiful and simple. There, in the high desert and with few distractions, I have prayed, meditated, and taken long walks in the desert. I have communed with the monastery cat, Madcap, and the monastery dog, Connor. I have supped with monks and broken my nightly fast in solitude. I have allowed my body and soul to return to their natural rhythms and I have found joy in just sitting, quietly. And, as a part of all of this, I have guided myself and been guided by Spirit through a great deal of reflection and recovery. I do not suggest that this is a tool for everyone. The point is, find tools that work for you.

You need not leave town as I have done to practice R&R, but you will need time alone and time away from the distractions of ordinary life. Anyone with a family knows there is a part of the self that gets easily lost within the vicissitudes of family life, however rich and rewarding that life may be. R&R is the richly rewarding experience of coming home to your-self, or more accurately, to the large and varied family that resides within the self. If you cannot get away, at least carve out some space and time for yourself. Go into a room and shut the door. Put a do-not-disturb sign out, if necessary. Take long walks by yourself and, preferably, somewhere in nature that is both beautiful and far enough from your neighborhood that you have an opportunity for solitude. Sit in your bathtub or hot tub for an extended period of time or sit in an empty church. In other words, do whatever it takes to find solitary, uninterrupted time. The cultivation of mind and spirit require solitude.

It is helpful to plan in some time for recovery and reflection early in the process of job search. Why? Because waiting only prolongs the healing; because the search itself can become absorbing; because you will carry your personal supply of internal junk with you until you realize that it is with you and let it go; because you need time to center yourself and relocate your internal gyroscope, your personal center of gravity.

Carmen has made a decision. For two years, she has been apprenticed to a shaman while, at the same time, making a living and maintaining a corporate image in a large brokerage firm. She has earned a good living, but it has taken a toll on her. Her work has been so demanding that, apart from her apprenticeship, she has had little life outside work. For a great while, she has felt that this work, fast paced, competitive, and completely oriented to the art and game of making money, is in conflict with what she values at a fundamental level, and this conflict has made her feel less than whole either at work or in her apprenticeship. She has decided to leave the brokerage firm.

Her co-workers and the firm's management are surprised, but not greatly so, when Carmen announces her intention to leave. Seen as highly competent, Carmen has also been viewed as different in mindset and lifestyle. When she gives notice, some of her peers shake their heads at her decision to leave a lucrative career for what she professes to be her destiny, unknown to her, but to which she has surrendered.

On Carmen's last day at the firm, she packs her few remaining personal possessions at the office and places a call to a friend who has agreed to drive her to the airport. Already packed for her trip, she stops at home long enough to collect her bags and leave a note for the woman who will water her plants and look after her place during her absence. Soon she is on a flight to New Mexico. She plans to stay in Taos, actually at a small ranch just outside of town, for three weeks. The woman with whom she will stay, a local *curandera* who is a friend of the shaman to whom she is apprenticed, understands that Carmen needs solitude and is happy to accommodate her.

Maria, the *curandera*, greets Carmen warmly when she arrives at the Ranch of the Half Moon. She shows her to a small, pretty guest cottage. Carmen quickly settles into a daily routine that is healing in its simplicity. She arises before dawn to greet the new day. Spending long hours hiking the ranch, she becomes intimate with arroyo and butte, tree and sagebrush, coyote and scrub jay. She meditates, leaning against a piñon pine, reflects on her life, and does simple ceremony. She lays, starts and tends the fire in her fireplace with intent and care and she prepares simple food for herself, eating it with more relish than she has for a long time, giving full attention to its smell, taste and texture. She seeks advice from the pinto ponies and mucks out their stalls with humility. At dusk, she greets the coming night as she has greeted the day. She spends long evenings sitting in a rocker on her small porch, searching the night sky for shooting stars with the same focus that she once searched for undervalued stocks. Maria teaches her how to make *posole* and cast-iron-skillet corn bread. The stars teach her how to transform herself.

Throughout all, she begins to remember what she has always known: everything is connected, the natural world is full of magic, synchronicity happens if she but remains observant, and her own intuition will guide her if she becomes silent and listens to the voice of her Higher Self. During her stay, Carmen spends several hours with Maria, talking over steaming mugs of herbal tea. She speaks of the job she has left, her fears, her dreams, and the stirrings within her. Maria listens and provides counsel during these *pláticas*, or heart-to-heart talks, serving as *consejera*, as counselor. Carmen learns that this is one of the traditional roles of the *curandera* and is grateful for Maria's compassion and earthy wisdom.

By the end of Carmen's three-week stay at the Ranch of the Half Moon, she feels grounded, centered, in touch with the natural world, at one with herself, and ready to step into her destiny, whatever it is.

Clearing The Organization

Once you leave an organization, for whatever reasons, it is good to clear yourself of it. I do not mean that you must sever all friendships and personal ties. *You* will know if you need to do that. But I do mean that it is important for you to cleanse your thoughts and emotions so you can move on. Think of this process as an extension of R&R.

A woman I know understood the importance of clearing work when she left an organization that had been important in shaping her as a professional. She held a "burning party" at her home. She invited guests, pulled out her non-compete agreement, which was about to expire, and got her house in order, physically and mentally. The non-compete agreement was not preventing her from making a living as a consultant, but it was a symbol, the last tie to her previous employer.

On the day the non-compete agreement expired, she had a party. The highlight of the event was the burning of the agreement. She is a practical and somewhat conservative sort of person. She did not don robes, prepare a huge bonfire for us to dance around, or ask her guests to chant anything. She lit her barbecue and we gathered around it. She talked about the organization and the many ways it had been a blessing in her life. She talked about friendships she had forged there. She talked about the need to move on. Then she burned the agreement in her barbecue. That burning held great emotional and spiritual significance for her.

This was a unique and personal ceremony. It also happened to be an excellent way to bridge the past and the future, to honor the important role her former employer had played in her career, and to clear any remnants of emotional charge attached to the employer and the non-compete agreement. Fire is the great transformer, clearing away the debris of what has been to make way for new possibilities.

Brigid left a company she had given heart and soul to for a very long time. The company was no longer a good fit for her and she prayed for both deliverance from it and the guidance necessary to know where she should be next. It could be said that her prayers were answered, although not quite as she had hoped. The parting was full of emotion, even though she knew it was for the best.

After a few days of emotional thrashing around, Brigid quickly settled into mental self-talk about the blessings she had received at the hands of the company. She certainly did not have purely positive feelings about her boss, but whenever negative feelings about him surfaced, she reminded herself of the many blessings she had received working for him. But she never got around to really confronting her anger and resentment. She finally realized that her energy was somewhat stuck where this issue was concerned and that she could not truly move on until she dealt with it in more than a superficial way. Brigid shared her feelings of being stuck with her career coach, who then gave her a *clearing* methodology.

Brigid did not come to the realization that she needed to clear the organization within the first month of her departure from the company, nor did she come to it within the first six months. It took longer. She finally faced it a full nine months after her departure. There was poetry in this, for she spent those nine months, in large measure, giving birth to herself through a process of reflection and personal transformation. That process was not complete for her, however, until she did some clearing work. Afterwards, she admitted it would have been nice to free up that energy sooner.

Why go to the trouble of doing the work to clear the organization? There is an old saying that one definition of craziness is continuing to do what you have *been* doing, but expecting to get different results. To the extent that this is true, crazy behavior is an abundant resource in the world! It reigns supreme among those who, though they have left working relationships, still carry an emotional charge about some people they have *related* to in those working relationships. Until they clear the emotional charge, they will continue to encounter, as if magnetically drawn to them, the same kinds of people. The names may change, the companies may change, but the same kinds of charged relationships continue, as if their lives are an old-fashioned long playing record with the stylus stuck in a groove that plays the same bit of music over and over again.

What happens when these people do some clearing work? Not only is the emotional charge diminished or eliminated, but they also get out of the groove they have been stuck in. When they do encounter someone remarkably similar to anyone they have carried that emotional charge with, they are energetically free to make different choices that lead to different outcomes.

There are many ways to get clear. Let me suggest one that has worked for my clients. It is based on the idea that to get clear you need to face your feelings about anyone associated with your previous employer who holds a "charge" for you, that is, anyone for whom you hold any residual feelings of anger, sadness or resentment.

I am not suggesting that the idea of clearing is only useful for purging yourself of feelings about the one or more people who, when you now think of them, invariably send your blood pressure up a few notches. While the technique is useful in clearing that particular negativity from your system, it is also useful in clearing anything that may obstruct a relationship you may want to retain.

Remember: one definition of craziness is continuing to do what you have been doing, but expecting to get different results. Clear the organization and free your energy for new possibilities.

Clearing Process
Technique I, Visualization
(Also Found On Accompanying CD)

1. Visualize yourself in a face-to-face meeting with your boss, your CEO, a peer, or anyone else in the organization who holds an emotional charge for you that you would like to transform.

2. Visualize that this person, one who has been important to you in some way, is contrite in describing the ways they have "wronged" you, how this may have made you feel, and how it may have affected your effectiveness. Visualize this person apologizing to you.

3. See yourself responding to the apology by confirming that you were affected by this person's treatment of you and articulating how you were affected. Accept this person's apology.

4. Acknowledge that you were also imperfect in your interactions with them. Describe what you now understand about *your part* in relating with this person of importance to you.

5. Next, affirm that all was not lost in the relationship and describe the blessings or gifts you received because of the relationship between the two of you.

6. Finally, forgive this person and ask their forgiveness for any wrongs you may have done them.

7. Now, envision a very large movie screen that you and this person turn to face. The two of you watch as scenes unfold of this person's future, scenes that depict abundance and blessings in all areas of life important to them.

8. Discuss the scenes as they pass before the two of you, each of you pleased by the goodness coming into this person's life. Allow these scenes to fade when there is a sense of completion.

9. Now notice that new scenes appear on the screen, ones that depict *your* future. Abundance and blessings rain upon your life in all areas important to you and you are supremely happy.

10. Again, discuss these scenes as they pass before the two of you, each of you pleased by the goodness coming into your life.

11. As these scenes finally fade, turn to one another and wish each other the best. Then say goodbye.

The more fully you can employ your five senses, the better you will experience this process. See the other person through your eyes. Hear what s/he and you have to say to one another. Allow yourself to feel any emotions or body sensations you may have during the experience. Notice whether there is a sour, sweet or bitter taste in your mouth. Detect any smells around you and the person with whom you are interacting.

It is important to make yourself comfortable and avoid distractions when you engage in this visualization. Brigid drew a warm bath, added bath salts and climbed in, resting against her bath pillow. Alternatively, you may want to sit comfortably in a chair, have the experience outdoors under a tree, or curl up in bed. Let the answering machine take your calls and make sure you are off-limits to children and pets during this exercise. I have found that it usually requires at least twenty minutes to fully engage in this visualization, but it may take more or less time for you. Do not rush it. Allow it to unfold.

Sometimes feelings about former bosses, colleagues, or others are complex enough that multiple visualizations per person are needed. As with divorce or other major relationship changes, you may find that you resolve some feelings only to discover, weeks or months later, that the same feelings, or even newly uncovered ones, surface. It is rather like peeling an onion. And it happens to many of us. Do not be concerned, just invoke the visualization again.

It is important to acknowledge feelings you need to dissipate about people you have experienced as friends and supporters. The clearing process is not used to vilify anyone. When we think of our parents, our siblings and other members of our family, most of us are willing to admit that we have experienced, through time, the full range of emotions towards them. Having felt anger, resentment, envy or jealousy does not diminish our feelings of love for them. Likewise, we have many feelings toward members of our work family and, as with our biological family, those we are the closest to are often those we have the full range of feelings towards. It is human to experience emotions that are sometimes contradictory during the course of long standing relationships.

It is also important to avoid censoring the process as you experience it. Your feelings are your feelings. Rightness and wrongness do not apply. Conformity to some kind of objective accuracy does not apply. They are your feelings, period. To clear yourself, you must first accept what is there to be cleared.

I do not suggest marathon sessions of clearing because they can be draining and can produce diminished results. Allow some time, a day or more, to pass between sessions. You want to experience the feeling of lightness each time you clear your feelings about a person.

Another effective method can be used in conjunction with or instead of the technique stated above.

Clearing Process
Technique II, Letter Writing

1. Get out your stationery and write a letter, which you are *not* going to

send, to anyone you need to clear. State your feelings about them, your feelings about your relationship with them, and the impact they have had on you. Be sure to mention not only the negative aspects of the relationship and your anger or resentment, but also the blessings they held for you.

2. Write until your hand, mind and heart have no more to say.

3. You can stop here, but this practice is even more powerful if you write a second letter, this one *from* the recipient of your first letter to *you*. In this letter, the sender writes to you what you would *like* to hear from them regarding your skills, your importance to the organization, the regrets the sender has about mistakes they have made, etc.

4. Write until you hand, mind and heart have no more to say.

5. Tear up, burn or otherwise destroy the letters. It is helpful to create a ritual around this. You may want to make a ceremony of it, complete with invocation, poetry or other readings, and the destruction of the letters while stating your release of your feelings and/or the person.

Many people feel a very powerful release from the act of physically putting pen to paper. To ensure that you do not simply arouse and stimulate your own anger or self-righteousness about the person to whom you are writing the letter, it is critical to perform the fifth step, that of letting go by physically letting go of the letters.

Clearing Process
Technique III, Breathing The Clearing

1. Sit comfortably in a meditative posture, eyes closed.

2. Focus on your breathing. Simply, gently focus on it. You may want to take a few deep breaths as you begin this exercise, but then return to comfortable, easy breathing. Allow your mid-section to gently expand as you breathe in and contract as you breathe out.

3. Now, allow a person you would like to clear to come to mind. Allow

yourself to notice any emotions you are having about this person as you visualize them.

4. Begin to *breathe in* the emotions you would like to clear about that person, be they anger, sadness, regret, or some other feeling.

5. Allow your body to positively transform these emotions in the brief moment between the in-breath and the out-breath.

6. As you *breathe out*, breathe freedom, spaciousness, love, compassion or whatever else you choose that is expansive *for both you and the other*.

7. Accept that the clearing will not take place fully in one or two breaths. Stay with this method of breathing for a time, allowing yourself to experience the gradual lightening, freshening, and clearing of your breathing.

This technique for clearing reminds me, a bit, of the Buddhist practice of tonglen. While I am not a practitioner of Buddhism and am not fully acquainted with the technique of tonglen, there does seem similarity to me in that both my breathing the clearing technique and tonglen seem to be about taking in the "unwanted," transforming it, and giving back the "wanted." For those of you interested in the practice of tonglen, I can recommend the work of Pema Chödrön[4], an American Buddhist nun who has a number of books and audiotapes you will find helpful.

Technique III is a very physical one. The whole body is involved. It is a very intimate way of clearing, because of this.

Clearing Process
Technique IV, Shamanic Journey

Note: If you are working with a shaman, you will receive guidance on your journey. If you are not working with a shaman, then you will need to guide yourself. The following instructions assume that you are taking a self-guided journey.

1. Create a quiet, undisturbed space for yourself. Make yourself comfortable by removing any clothing that is constraining, distracting or impedes your breathing.

2. If you have not already done so, empty your bladder. Shamanic journeys have a way of filling the bladder. Start out with an empty bladder and you will be more comfortable.

3. Light candles, dim the lights, and/or close the window shades. If you have a sage, sage blend, sweet grass, or other smudge stick, honor your process and purify the environment by smudging the room and yourself.[5]

4. Put on facilitative music. You will find a tape or CD of shamanic drumming[6] to be extremely helpful because its beat will facilitate your entry into an altered state of consciousness. If you have a remote control device, cue up the music and set the volume levels, but do not begin the music until you begin the journey process.

5. Lie down for your journey, legs raised on pillows so your back is firmly pressed against the floor (or mattress if you are on a bed). Place a pillow under your head if you need it. Cover yourself with a light blanket, as this work tends to lower body temperature.

6. Before starting the journey, program yourself to enter into a journey state that will inform you of the clearing needed and will facilitate the clearing process. Frame a question to express this intent, such as "Who are the people I need to clear at this time and what is the best way for me to accomplish this clearing?"

7. Also, invoke the presence of what is helpful and good during the process. You may find it helpful to mentally place a white light around you.

8. Begin by practicing shamanic breathing for a few minutes. Breath in to the count of four, allowing your belly to expand with the in-breath. Hold the breath to a count of seven. Release the breath, contracting your belly naturally, to a count of eight. Pause briefly before the next in-breath.

9. As you return to normal breathing, begin to systematically relax. Start with your toes, move up to your arch, heel and ankle, proceed to your shins and thighs, and so on until you have relaxed your entire body.

10. If you have delayed the beginning of the music because you have a remote control device with you, start the music now.

11. Feel your body melt into the floor, like warm liquid spreading outward. Then begin to feel your body lighten until it, of its own accord, begins to ascend.

12. Know that a portal into another realm awaits you and, in a relaxed and accepting state, be aware of it becoming visible to you.

13. Pass through the portal.

14. Allow your Higher Self, your guidance, or your allies to guide you on your journey. Avoid any attempt to consciously orchestrate the process. Instead, surrender to the process itself.

15. When your journey has concluded, pass back through the portal and into ordinary reality. Take whatever time you need to relax and integrate the experience before arising.

16. Record the experience as soon as possible. Shamanic journeys, or parts of them, can be both complex and ephemeral, so a recording of the experience before parts of it vaporize in the light of ordinary reality is useful. Further, meaning and significance may unfold for you over the coming days or weeks.

The shamanic journey is a method used for centuries to expand con-sciousness, facilitate healing, and gain guidance. These journeys take place in an altered state of consciousness. Shamanic breathing, deep relaxation, and drumming facilitate access to this state in the clearing method using shamanic journey. The shamanic journey is typically undertaken because the journeyer has an important question or need for specific information and/or guidance. In the clearing technique using shamanic journey, the issue around which the journey revolves is the need for clearing.

During a shamanic journey, the journeyer may travel, undertake quests, ascend or descend to realms not accessed during normal states of consciousness, and may come to new understandings and learnings about his/her life and life's path. This is deep work and, because of that, it is extremely helpful to be guided on shamanic journeys by a shaman. The shaman will not only create sacred space for the journey and guide the journeyer through the pre-journey activities, but will also "hold the space," that is, maintain a protective, sacred energetic atmosphere throughout the process.

Clearing Through Dreams

Another form of clearing can happen during sleep and the process of dreaming. Because this process happens spontaneously, orchestrated by the subconscious mind, I have not referred to clearing through dreams as a *technique*.

Once you have begun to consciously examine your career or engage in a job search, particularly if you have already left an organization, you may find that the number and/or content of your dreams changes. In fact, some people find that this begins even before they physically leave the organization, a kind of precursor to the act of leaving.

If you have never recorded your dreams, this is a good time to start. While some people find it helpful to keep a pad of paper and pen next to the bed to record their dreams if they awaken during the night, I do not personally use this approach for the simple reason that the act of scribbling notes brings me up to a thoroughly awakened state, making it difficult to return to sleep. I do, however, take a few minutes upon waking in the morning to allow my dreams to settle in my memory before arising. Once the feet hit the floor, the previous night's dreams can be gone from mind if there is not a conscious attempt to ground them.

Recording your dreams is one way to facilitate your memory of them. It is as if the *subconscious* mind responds to your making an effort to record your dreams by treating your *conscious* mind as one that takes its dream state seriously. It, therefore, supports your conscious mind by increasing your ability to remember your dreams, and remember them more fully and robustly, than in the past. Record your dreams as soon as possible after awakening to maximize the possibility of capturing as much as possible.

Brigid found that her dreams took on a new intensity after she left her job. One night, in particular, she had a dream that left her feeling light and free upon awakening. In this dream, she found herself leaving a large building. In her hand, she carried a piece of paper on which was written the names, titles and work phone numbers of several of the most difficult people with whom she had worked at the company. Brigid walked the streets of a strange city, endlessly, holding that piece of paper.

Finally, she came to a large lake. Over the lake, the sky was brilliantly cast in shades of deep purple, crimson and gold as an otherworldly sun, larger than the sun in waking reality, set. A doe wandered out of the woods adjoining the lake and came to stand next to her.

"Step into the lake," the doe spoke to her, mind to mind.

Brigid found herself afraid to step into the lake, not knowing how deep it might be, and she felt resentful of the doe's suggestion. She might *need* these phone numbers and they would be lost if she found herself in deep water. But the doe looked upon her with such soft eyes that she began to soften, too. Further, the lake itself glowed and shimmered in a thoroughly inviting way. Perhaps it was safe to venture in.

Brigid took a tentative step into the lake. The water was warm. She ventured further within and found the water enveloping her, like large and loving arms. She held her own arm aloft, not wanting the piece of paper to get wet. But the water was so inviting she surrendered to it, allowing herself, and the piece of paper, to become fully immersed.

Brigid watched as the ink on the paper, still clutched in her hand, began to dissolve. When there was no more ink left on the paper, she let it drift away from her. Then she swam, as effortlessly as a dolphin, even though she knew that she could not normally swim. The joy and freedom of swimming felt as a gentle urging within her and she explored the lake, swimming under the water with no impediment to her breathing, for a long time. She traveled with schools of fish, saw beautiful lake flora and even came upon an old, wrecked boat at the lake's bottom. She thought of exploring the boat, but decided she could return another time to do so. When she emerged from the lake, Brigid found that she glowed and shimmered just as did the lake.

When she awoke from this dream in the early hours of morning, Brigid rummaged through her nightstand for a piece of paper and pen. Still dreamy from sleep, she recorded the dream before it could drift away from her waking mind.

Whether through one—or all—of the techniques just mentioned, through a burning ritual like that my acquaintance employed to signify the end of her non-compete agreement, or via some method of your own device you tailor to fit your personal needs, what you accomplish from a clearing practice is the joyous untying of a rope that has impeded your forward movement. You may continue relationships with some people you have cleared, if it is appropriate and of mutual benefit, but I can guarantee those relationships will be changed for your personal betterment, subtly or obviously. You may never again see or have a relationship with other people you have cleared, but the ongoing internal relationship with them based on your memories will be forever changed as a result of the clearing practice.

What can happen when you do not do some form of clearing? Sometimes you keep meeting the people you have not cleared, over and over again. They may have different names and they may take different forms, but they will seem surprisingly familiar.

Jim's parting of the ways with the company had not exactly been pleasant, but it was, in many ways, a relief. For five years, he had been CFO of a high profile, high growth computer software company. Jim had played a major role in the company's success and the fact of this was public knowledge. But when market conditions sent the company on a downward spiral, the CEO implemented strategies that emphasized expediency over ethics and profits over people. Jim believed the company could successfully address market conditions and be profitable while retaining ethical standards and treating its employees fairly. What constituted ethics had been an ongoing debate between Jim and the CEO. The fair treatment of employees had been less an issue until the CEO decided to lay off 10% of the workforce with little notice and no separation pay. After six months of deepening rift between himself and the CEO, the CEO asked Jim to leave.

It did not take Jim long to find another position. Jim felt the best way to get past his disappointment over the company he had left was to quickly take a new job with a company more in keeping with his values. His new job, this time as CFO for a computer peripherals company, started off well. His new boss, the CEO, was a woman by the name of Theresa, who liked to be called Terry. There was something ironic about this because his former boss, named Terrance, also went by the name Terry. Jim believed this was both the beginning and the end of any similarity between them.

He was wrong. While his new boss talked of ethical standards, fair and equitable treatment of employees, customer satisfaction, profits with principles, and open communications, Jim quickly found she was more interested in a public persona that touted these ideas than in their private corporate practice. Jim felt he had made strategic and tactical errors in the way he had handled the situation with the previous employer and did not want to repeat them. He worked to influence the CEO with logic and an appeal to find win-win solutions. He pointed out the risks involved in not matching public persona with corporate reality. The CEO patronized him for three months, ignored him for two more, and fired him at the end of six months.

Jim left the company feeling not just disappointed, but also bitter. What had gone wrong? Was every job going to be a *déjà vu* nightmare of the previous job? Perhaps he should have examined his feelings about Terry #1 before taking a job with Terry #2.

Accepting Yourself

Ah, accepting yourself. Now we get down to it. Those who have mastered this one, go on to the next section. However, if you would not quite use the word *mastery* here, perhaps you might want to read on. You may have just been summarily discharged from a company that employed you for the past fifteen years, feel disillusioned, disheartened and, basically, lower than the average worm. You mutter to yourself that this writer who knows nothing of how you feel now wants to talk with you about accepting yourself when your self-acceptance is at an all time low. As a matter of fact, she does. There is no better time to get clear about self-acceptance.

If you are in such a predicament, how did you get there? I am not asking how you came to be in job search and/or a re-examination of your career, I am asking how you came to feel this unaccepting of self. Only you can answer that question, but there do seem to be patterns about this in our society. If you grew up in a home that was wholly and completely giving of unconditional love, raise your hands. Not many hands rose out there, I will wager. I am not suggesting you blame your parents. In fact, a bit of compassion for your parents will help on the road to self-acceptance. Your parents did the best they could within their model of the world.

The point is that most of us grew up with some form of conditional regard. If we cleaned our rooms, we were good girls and boys. If we did not clean our rooms, we were either naughty or inconsiderate or both. We were praised if we got good grades or at least what constituted good grades for us. If our grades slipped, we probably did not get much praise. To one degree or another, most of us internalized that conditional regard. We are not victims and no one is to blame. This is simply the way it was for most of us.

To further complicate matters, our culture has long supported the utilitarian concept that what is useful is good and what is not useful is, if not bad, at least not as good as what is useful. Within this framework, it is no surprise that the arts struggle while commercial business thrives.

Most of us have internalized this utilitarian approach in at least a couple of ways. First, we have social stature to the extent that we have been found useful in life and someone is willing to pay for that utility. Many of us have taken this further and have embraced the notion that the amount of pay we earn is, if not in direct proportion, at least related to our worth. There is a great deal of societal support for this thinking, so there is no need to beat ourselves up for it. Second, many of us become highly identified with our jobs or careers and, frequently, we even extend this identification to the company for which we work. "I'm Director of Operations for XYZ Corporation," we say within the first five minutes after being introduced to a stranger at a party. Michael Jordan has not just been a superstar basketball player, he has been a superstar basketball player for the Chicago Bulls, and both Jordan and the Bulls have, somehow, heightened their stature in the process.

I am not sure which of these two culturally imbued qualities within us—the tendency to administer conditional regard to ourselves or the tendency to become intensely identified with professions and/or companies—affects us worse when we suddenly find ourselves in job search. I *can* say that many people are shocked to learn how profoundly they have identified with their professions and/or organizations and how much like having the rug pulled out from under them they feel when they leave a job, *even when* they, themselves, walk away. This is often one of the first blows to self. Later they frequently feel unsettled about not having something tangible to point to that demonstrates worth through utility. There is a cultural predisposition towards believing that we *are* what we *do*.

Facing either or both of these can create very real discomfort and can become the path to self-acceptance. Once you either abandon or lose your identity with career or company, you are thrown back on yourself to determine who you are and who you want to be. It is a great opportunity for not only recreating and redefining yourself, but also for developing a deep knowing that there is something Divine within you that is perfect just as it is, without societal definitions or identifications.

As for conditional regard, once you have surrendered the ongoing, or even occasional, regard you grant yourself through the *possession* of a job, you discover that self-regard and possession of anything do not belong in the same sentence. You have not been good because you have been employed and you are not bad if you are no longer employed. Looking within your own heart, you find there is a fundamental quality of goodness in you that has nothing to do with the conditions in which you find yourself or, for that matter, have created for yourself.

You may be helped along the way by asking yourself some very simple questions:

- Who am I, anyway, beyond jobs, titles and roles?
- What do I stand for?
- How do I know myself at the core of my being?
- What draws forth in me my highest and produces the highest good for me and those around me?
- How do I know that I am fundamentally good?
- How do I carry myself in society without the societal crutch of being known for a position I have held and/or a company for whom I have worked?

Daniel has held senior management positions for several companies over that past twenty years, positions ranging from Director of Sales and Marketing to General Manager and, ultimately, to President. Within the past year and a half, Daniel has begun to feel empty. He has a wonderful, supportive wife and three delightful children. He has a home in the city and a cabin in the mountains. He has set career goals for himself and he has met them. Now what?

Daniel has come to a career coach because he finds himself vaguely dissatisfied, vaguely on edge. It has always seemed to him that his positions with companies have come to him with little effort on his part. They have virtually fallen into his lap. He has never had to examine who he is or what he wants to do. He has been so busy with work and family for the past twenty years that he has spent little time either by himself or pursuing interests that are particular to him. In fact, he no longer *has* many interests apart from his work and family life.

The career coach asks Daniel who he is, stripped of the title, the job, the wife, the children, the city home, the cabin, the stock portfolio, his daily five mile runs, his college degrees, his awards, and all of his other roles and possessions. Daniel is struck dumb by the question. His face tenses noticeably and he admits that the question makes him uncomfortable.

"Who and what *are* you, without all of that," the career coach asks

---

again. Daniel sits quietly for a time. He fidgets in his seat. He looks down at his hands.

"Can you give me a hint?" he asks the career coach, with an uncomfortable little smile.

"I'm not going to help you with *this* one," she replies. "The answer is within you."

Daniel sighs a deep sigh. Even though this is his first meeting with the coach, he knows something about her work from the business friend who has referred him to her. He has been told that she will not do all of the work for him, will not give him platitudes, has a built-in dung detector, and will both stay focused herself and keep him focused on what is critical and fundamental. *She's certainly doing those things*, he thinks to himself.

The career coach works with Daniel to nudge, from both his conscious and subconscious minds and both his left and right brains, that which will help him find the answers to her questions. When the meeting is over, Daniel leaves perplexed, but realizing that she has struck upon the root issue that has caused his feelings of emptiness and dissatisfaction. *Who am I, after all*, he wonders. *Could this really be about knowing who I am...and accepting myself?*

You may find it helpful to the development of self-acceptance to practice some self-guided imagery. Here are a few suggestions:

Accepting Yourself
Technique I, Returning To The Beginning
(Also Found On Accompanying CD)

1. Get as comfortable as you wish to be, close your eyes, and concentrate on your breathing just long enough to sink into relaxation.
2. In your mind, take yourself back to a time when you were in your mother's womb. You are warm, you are fed, and you have everything you need. You accept that you deserve all that comes to you, simply because you are *you*.

3. Now, take yourself forward, to the time of your birth. You arrive in the world exultant to be alive. You are cooed over by the beings around you. You are wrapped in warm cloth. Perhaps you are taken to your mother's breast. You see yourself as you are seen by your parents—perfect in every way and perfectly loved. You are small, helpless, and innocent. You can do nothing wrong and are loved unconditionally.

4. Now *see* that feeling of being loved unconditionally…as a small ball of golden light.

5. Move that small ball of light forward through time until you have brought it into the present. Allow the ball of light to expand until it becomes as large as a basketball. Fold your arms around it, pulling it in, towards the middle part of your body.

6. Let the ball of light permeate your skin and radiate throughout you.

7. When you are ready, return to normal awareness, stopping to feel the warmth, resonance, and brightness of that unconditional love within you.

Accepting Yourself
Technique II, Letting Go Of Your Roles
(Also Found On Accompanying CD)

1. Get as comfortable as you wish to be, close your eyes, and concentrate on your breathing just long enough to sink into relaxation.

2. See yourself as you are, holding all the roles you have taken on in this life. Allow yourself to *feel* these roles, viscerally, and allow yourself to sense your feelings about *yourself* within these roles. Hear the words you use in your daily life. Notice any other sensations that you associate with your roles. A smell or taste may come to you.

3. Allow yourself to stand apart from that part of you that lives within these roles, watching and sensing—in perfect comfort—the one who lives within these roles. As you watch the self-who-lives-within-roles,

consciously ask that self to allow the professional role to drop away, as if removing a piece of clothing and allowing it to fall to the floor. Sense that self without the role of professional.

4. Now, consciously ask the self-who-lives-within-roles to allow the role of daughter or son to drop away. In perfect comfort, sense that self without the role of child.

5. Now, consciously allow another role to drop away, perhaps the role of spouse or partner. Again, sense that self without this role, maintaining the feeling of perfect comfort.

6. If the self-who-lives-within-roles is a parent, consciously ask that self to let the role of parent to drop away and watch that self without this role.

7. Continue to ask the self-who-lives-within-roles to let the many roles drop away, one at a time. These may include such roles as civic leader, responsible homeowner, church member, athlete, or nurturer of the hearth.

8. Once all the roles of the self-who-lives-within-roles have dropped away, notice, as the-one-who-stands-apart-in-perfect-comfort, the self who remains. What does this person look like? What is this person's sound and quality of voice? What feelings are aroused by the self-whose-roles-have-dropped-away? Are any sensations of taste or smell associated with that self? Has that self changed in any physical way, devoid of the roles?

9. Place a warm golden light filled with love, caring, and acceptance on the crown of the head of the self who is now devoid of roles. Allow the golden light to enter and permeate the body of that self. Notice the light as it continues to move through the body and strengthen with every breath taken by that self. Become aware as the light throbs with the heartbeat of that self and intensifies to the point of extending down into the ground, up through the head and out from all parts of the body, touching the world around the self even as it continues to intensify within that self.

10. As the self-who-stands-apart—remaining in absolute comfort—merge into the self of the one who is now devoid of roles. Sense the luminous quality, warmth, resonance, and total integration of that self.
11. When you are ready, return to normal awareness, retaining the self-acceptance of the self without roles.

Accepting Yourself
Technique III, Sensing Perfection
(Also Found On Accompanying CD)

1. Get as comfortable as you wish to be, close your eyes, and concentrate on your breathing just long enough to sink into relaxation.
2. Maintain an awareness of the self-you-are-today with your personality, physical attributes, and all other qualities of self and personal characteristics intact.
3. Bring to mind a Being of Divine Perfection, whether that is a Spiritual Master, God, your own Higher Self or whatever else personifies perfection for you.
4. Invite that Being, that personification of perfection, to join you now. Take some time to sense the qualities of perfection that radiate from this Being.
5. Request that this Being provide you with a *physical* manifestation, *outside* itself, that represents the fullness and quality of its perfection.
6. Once you experience this physical manifestation, request that this Being allow you to possess this manifestation of perfection, knowing that this Being will, joyfully and with love, grant your request.
7. Accept this gift of perfection and notice its qualities, allowing it to transform itself in any manner that will allow it—effortlessly and easily—to be merged with you. Once this has happened, allow yourself to embody it. Feel the radiant energy of pure perfection within you, knowing that you have been given a gift of priceless value and that it will remain with you for all time.

8. Create a personal intent to fully integrate this perfection *now*, within you, and to honor it in all ways that are significant to you.

9. When you are ready, return to normal awareness, embodying the perfection within. Allow yourself some time to sense any shifts in your awareness brought about by this gift.

Shadow

There are entire books written on the subject of self-acceptance and I am only touching on it here. But I cannot leave the topic without broaching the subject of the "shadow side." While there are many ways to look at the shadow within, and many ways about which it has been written, for our purposes I will define the shadow side of our being simply: it is all we have denied and/or suppressed within ourselves. This definition is inclusive and covers what we might view as the positive within as well as what we might view as the negative within.

As children, we are encouraged to be "good little girls and boys." If we have a plethora of toys, we are encouraged to share them when what we often prefer to do is hoard them, keeping them to ourselves for our own pleasure and use. Many of us then learn to suppress the part of us we are told is greedy and ungenerous. That part of us becomes part of the shadow side.

Likewise, if we find at an early age that we are above average in intelligence or have unusual talents or skills, we are often encouraged to downplay these aspects of ourselves in favor of seeming to be "just like everyone else." We may have been told that the full expression of these parts of ourselves will make us appear arrogant or will intimidate others. We may have discovered on our own that their expression elicits envy in others. Many of us then learn to suppress or downplay our own strengths. Those parts of us also become part of the shadow side.

If we are to become fully alive, fully functioning human beings, we must acknowledge and honor *all* that is within us. This means, in part, that we must access the shadow sides of our own natures, learn from them, come to terms with them, see them as a part of our own humanity, work with them, and use them to our advantage. What happens when we do not do this is all too clear.

Many of us have worked with people who have unacknowledged shadow. Some of these people do incredible damage within organizations because they cannot accept that they can make mistakes. If an error is found, they point a finger at someone else. "I didn't do it, he did/the system did/the other department did," they say in self-defense. Yet, one sign of a fully adult human being is the ability to recognize, accept and correct our own mistakes.

Others who have not acknowledged their shadow sides work within a cloud of mystery. They collect information, but do not share it. They always seem to have an agenda. Still others hide their singular skills. Sometimes they do this with the belief that it is more important to support team effort. Sometimes they do this fearing that management will single them out for greater responsibility, making them feared or disliked by their peers. Sometimes they are unaware they are hiding their own, magnificent light. Anyone whose performance reviews have included comments like, "has not worked up to full potential" has probably relegated at least some of their ability to the shadow side.

It is often easier to see the shadow in another than it is to see our own. If you have taken one or more psychological inventories or personality tests, you have probably begun to get a glimpse of your shadow side. It may feel as if you have been walking a city street for a long succession of cloudy days and now find yourself walking the same street with the sun shining brightly. You are startled to see someone walking with you and realize that you have noticed, through your peripheral vision, your own shadow.

Apart from psychological inventories that assist you in understanding yourself, how do you access the shadows within? One of the easiest ways is to take heed of everyone and everything that elicits strong feelings. If you have had a strong, stubborn, authoritarian boss who annoyed you beyond measure, you might want to look for those attributes within. If you have been fascinated by the lives of great artists, philosophers or leaders, you might want to access those qualities within yourself. If you have a strong and automatic reaction to the greed of big business, the thoughtlessness of our country's use of natural resources, the occasional misuse of power perpetrated by members of law enforcement, then you should take note and look within for the shadow of these things that dwells within you.

You may have heard that everyone and everything in our lives is like a mirror to us, reflecting our own substance, our own persona, and both the best and worst in us. It is a sure bet that whatever or whomever pushes your buttons is mirroring something for you! These are opportunities, served up by the Universe, to examine some aspect of yourself you may be avoiding. Think of those mirrors reflecting the shadow in you as postcards from the Universe. It is easier to see into ourselves when we can see a mirror reflection.

This is not simply a matter of purging the negative we find within and celebrating the positive. Years ago, as I participated in a guided imagery designed to help me integrate the various aspects of myself, I found myself struck by the power of integrating what I viewed as my negative shadow. If I could identify an archetype, like Hitler, who could kill mercilessly and if I could find something of that ruthlessness within, how could it serve me? I was able to find within myself a part that could kill without thought or guilt should I need to do so in order to protect myself or someone else. It was good to acknowledge and honor that ability...and have the strength to admit it.

Likewise, if I could identify an archetype, like Rudolf Nureyev, who was strong, talented, and graceful and if I could find something of those attributes within myself, how could it serve me? I was able to find within myself a woman who could, at least symbolically, dance among many worlds with strength and grace.

The object, then, is to unearth and own these parts of you. To some extent, this is a process of becoming amused with and accepting of the parts of you that are not, after all, of the highest. Once you have done this, you can begin the process of alchemy, which transforms them into something meaningful and useful in your life. If, for instance, you find that behind the loving, accepting exterior lies a shadow that can be alarmingly and irrationally prejudiced, then *just acknowledging* that fact helps you catch yourself in the act of experiencing those prejudicial feelings. And when you catch yourself in the act, you can dig deeper, to find what is at the root of that feeling and begin to disarm it. Or you can simply observe the feeling, as if standing outside it in curiosity, and then make a conscious choice to transform the feeling.

Where the positive shadow is concerned, you can accept that you are, after all, more than you have acknowledged and, again, begin the process of alchemy to transform what lies within into something that can find expression in the world. You can ask yourself what you are so afraid of, what inspires you to block your talents and gifts. Sometimes that beginning question takes you to some very deep places within, leading to deeper and deeper questions that ultimately unlock the door to fabulous self-expression and creativity.

Another way to access the shadow within is through dreams. As you begin to attend to your dreams, record them, and allow them to elicit memories and thoughts, you may find evidence of your own shadow side within them. This may take the form of people and events that are troubling, make you afraid, or even disgust you. You may also find yourself saying and doing things in your dreams that seem surprising and even foreign to you. I encourage you to consciously look for signs of the shadow within your dreams. When you bring the hidden, the suppressed, and the denied up to the level of consciousness, you can begin to apply the alchemy to transform it.

Finally, a very useful way to explore the shadow side within is to examine myths and archetypes found in stories and expressed in life. As you examine the characteristics of these myths and archetypes, you may find that they evoke thoughts and feelings within you.

Following are suggestions for helping you bring light to what has been in shadow and to learn from it.

Discovering And Working With The Shadow Side

1. What **people** in your life, past or present, elicit strong thoughts and feelings, either positive or negative, when you call them to mind?
   - What is there about those people that strongly attracts or repels you?
   - Summarize this in groups of words and/or phrases that may be associated with each person.
   - What is your reaction to what you have identified?
   - Can you admit to or image these words/phrases in relation to yourself?
   - How?
   - Do feelings of embarrassment or shame surface?
   - Do memories from childhood, adolescence or early adulthood surface?
   - If so, write down and/or simply reflect on these memories.
   - Have you repressed or denied parts of yourself that relate, in any way, to these memories?
   - Can you find some way in which the qualities expressed in the words/phrases and in your memories can be used, in some positive form, to your advantage?
   - If so, imagine yourself, at some future point, fully using this quality, effortlessly, skillfully and to the advantage of both yourself and others.
2. What images, people, and events from recent **dreams** evoke strong positive or negative thoughts or feelings?
   - What is there about these images, people and events that strongly

attracts or repels you?

- Summarize this in groups of words and/or phrases that may be associated with them.
- What is your reaction to what you have identified?
- Can you admit to or image these words/phrases in relation to yourself?
- How?
- Do feelings of embarrassment or shame surface?
- Do memories from childhood, adolescence or early adulthood surface?
- If so, write down and/or simply reflect on these memories.
- Have you repressed or denied parts of yourself that relate, in any way, to these memories?
- Can you find some way in which the qualities expressed in the words/phrases and in your memories can be used, in some positive form, to your advantage?
- If so, imagine yourself, at some future point, fully using this quality, effortlessly, skillfully and to the advantage of both yourself and others.

3. What **myths and archetypes** attract or repel you for the positive symbology they represent for you? What myths and archetypes attract or repel you for the negative symbology they represent for you?

- What is there about these myths and archetypes that strongly attracts or repels you, positively or negatively?
- Summarize this in groups of words and/or phrases that may be associated with them.
- What is your reaction to what you have identified?
- Can you admit to or image these words/phrases in relation to yourself?
- How?
- Do feelings of embarrassment or shame surface?
- Do memories from childhood, adolescence or early adulthood surface?

- If so, write down and/or simply reflect on these memories.
- Have you repressed or denied parts of yourself that relate, in any way, to these memories?
- Can you find some way in which the qualities expressed in the words/phrases and in your memories can be used, in some positive form, to your advantage?
- If so, imagine yourself, at some future point, fully using this quality, effortlessly, skillfully and to the advantage of both yourself and others.

It is not as if you can identify and work through all aspects of your shadow side once and for all, finishing as if it were an assignment to be completed. Your external shadow reappears on any sunny day. Your internal shadow stays with you as well. But to the extent that you acknowledge it, honor it, and work to transform and use it, you can live with it effectively. It also helps to maintain a healthy sense of humor. You are, after all, human. At the end of the day, that is what accepting yourself is all about.

Homework

It is a good idea to do your homework when planning a trip. Some of that homework, if you are smart, addresses not only the possible travel destination, but also what kind of traveler you are. Some people prefer to travel only within the confines of their home country, while others like to travel more broadly, sometimes to remote locations. When traveling abroad, some people insist on having a good grasp of the local language, while others are perfectly comfortable with a phrase book and hand gestures. Some folks want to stay in luxury hotels while others are quite happy camping out. These things really depend on one's preferences, life style, budget and comfort level with the unknown.

The same holds true for your job search journey or career exploration expedition. A little homework early in the career exploration process can help you identify just which kinds of destinations are suitable for you are which are not. These things are not carved in stone. You can change your mind as *you* change during your journey. But a little clarification about who you are *up front* can save you a great deal of grief later, just as the traveler who really prefers to stay in five star hotels will save herself considerable discomfort if she admits that *before* agreeing to the backpacking trip with overnights at hostels.

From Strengths To "Just Say No"

Create the following four lists:
- My strengths: what I am good at in both my work and personal lives;
- What I really like to do (which may or may not coincide with strengths) in both my work and personal lives;
- My weaknesses: what I'm not as good at in both my work and personal lives;
- What I would just as soon never have to do again (which may or may not coincide with weaknesses) in both my work and personal lives.

These lists will begin to help you determine what feeds your soul and what does not. They will help you discern what to pursue actively, what to consider improving, and what to avoid.

Boundaries

What are your boundaries, that is, what are the limits of what you will or will not accept, in all of the areas important to you? These might include:
- Geography: part of a metro area; state; region; country
- Pay: minimum base; commission structure; total compensation
- Type of work

- Employee/Self Employed
- Full or Part-time work
- Culture of company/behavioral characteristics of boss and/or peers
- Management style you will/will not accept from your boss
- An office of your own; a cubicle; a room at home devoted to your business; a part of the dining room table devoted to your business

If you do not know what your boundaries are, you may accept something that just does not work for you, blind-sided in a moment of thrill at being handed an opportunity. If you are working with a coach, s/he will need to understand your boundaries in order to help you fulfill your intent and stay on purpose.

The People In My Life

Create the following three lists of people in your life:
- Business and Professional Contacts
- Friends and Family
- Everyone Else

While you may not want or need to network with *all* these people, just creating the lists begins to help you crystallize *who* is actually in your network, from close contacts to those on the periphery. My experience is that most people set about to create these lists only to find that once they have made the first pass at it, they continue to think of people not on the lists and keep adding names.

Get creative with this. The *Business and Professional Contacts* category not only should include people with whom you currently work and with whom you have worked in the past, but also your professional peers in other organizations, contacts from professional societies, vendors, and customers. The *Friends and Family* list should include not only those friends and acquaintances you see regularly, but also those you may not have contacted for some time. The *Everyone Else* list might include neighbors you know only slightly, the man behind the counter at the dry cleaner, and the clerks you have been chatting with at the grocery store for the past five years.

My Ideal Job

1. Take a fresh look at who you are and what you want for yourself in the world of work. Examine your knowledge base, your experience and your skills. Review the *From Strengths To "Just Say No"* and *Boundaries* exercises. What do you love to do? What have you done that you would not wish to repeat? What kind of people do you want to experience in the world of work? What are your boundaries? What work environment do you want for yourself?

2. Now, using this information, describe in written form (pen and paper or on the computer) your first month in your ideal job. Use the present tense in this piece of writing. If you choose to do so, define the circumstances that led to this opportunity. Where are you, geographically? Describe all aspects of the physical surroundings in which you work. Describe the people you encounter. How do you feel? How are you dressed? What are the most important things you are charged with accomplishing during your first year in this ideal job? Are they a stretch, but doable? How do you feel about them? Describe your first day on the job, your first week, and the subsequent three weeks. How do you feel at the end of the first month? How do you feel about the coming eleven months?

3. Once you have written your thoughts and feelings, re-read it. Is there anything you would like to change? If so, change it by rewriting it. Do you feel pleased and excited about the possibilities? If not, rethink your ideal job. Do you feel sufficiently challenged without being overwhelmed? Adjust the job and your duties as a result. Once you have done this, enter your own story by using your mind and all your physical senses.

4. Set your intent on what you have created.

5. Put aside this exercise. Revisit it after twenty-four hours. Are you still happy with it? Does it still speak to you? If not, make any changes necessary. Revisit your ideal job after a week and after a month. Again, make changes to make the ideal job more consistent with who you now are, a week or month after your first writing. Again, set your intent.

6. Remain flexible about your ideal job. Know that you can change the story line and reset your intent whenever it is appropriate to do so. If, in re-examining your ideal job, you feel flutterings of fear, allow yourself to examine the source of your fear. Have you created an ideal job that is unattainable or are you simply afraid of stepping into your own dream? Allow feelings of trust in the Universe and love for yourself to supersede any feelings of self doubt or fear, as is appropriate.

Finding An Internal *Yes* And An Internal *No*

You will be faced with many options and choices during your journey. It is important to explore them using every tool your rational mind has at its disposal *and* every tool your intuitive mind has at its disposal. We all have an internal guidance system that will, if we ask it, give us a sense of whether or not any particular choice or option is a good idea or bad idea. But before you can make use of that guidance system for any particular question, you need to know what an internal *yes* and *no* are.

1. Think of a time when you needed to make a decision or choice, you made the decision, and it turned out to be a good one.

    ✦ You did your homework, that is, you used all of the resources your rational mind had to offer. For instance, you may have gathered information on the Internet about a company, interviewed with half a dozen people there, and talked with your stockbroker about the company's fiscal viability. Or you may have been asked by a boyfriend to enter into an exclusive relationship with him. You gathered information, over time, about the quality of your relationship with him by dating and spending time with him.

+ Your rational thinking process told you to go ahead.

+ You also checked your internal guidance system. It told you visually (you saw something), auditorily (you heard something), kinesthetcally (you felt something), olfactoraly (you smelled something), or gustatorily (you tasted something) that it was the right decision.

+ You made the decision to go forward and, as it unfolded in time, it was the right decision.

+ What signal(s) did you get from your internal guidance system? Did you see a green light? Did you hear an internal *yes*? Did you feel warmth in your solar plexus or in the center of your chest? Did you smell something that was remarkably like a hot apple pie fresh from the oven or the scent of roses? Did you have the sensation of sweetness in your mouth? Whichever signal your internal guidance system gave you, recall it.

2. Now think of a time when you were posed with a decision or choice, decided against this choice, and found you had made the right decision.

+ You used all your rational decision-making processes and felt it was not a good choice for you.

+ Then you checked with your internal guidance system and got a visual, auditory, kinesthetic, olfactory, or gustatory message advising you not to go forward.

+ You made the decision not to go forward and, as it unfolded in time, it was the right decision.

+ What signal did you get from your internal guidance system?

You *need* to know what an internal *yes* and an internal *no* is for you so that at any time you are faced with a decision, you can check out the wisdom of going forward or not with both your rational thinking system *and* your internal guidance system. The time to know what your internal guidance system provides for you in the way of affirmatives or negatives is *not* the moment when you have the question, but *before* you need the information!

For What Am I Not Forgiving Myself?

We have all done things in our lives that were not of the highest. Perhaps you have made mistakes you have later regretted, even serious mistakes that had major consequences and led to feelings of guilt. There is nothing wrong with guilt, providing you treat it like an internal alarm clock. The purpose of an alarm clock is to get your attention, to wake you up. The appropriate thing to do when an alarm clock has claimed your attention is to turn it off and get on with your day.

Where mistakes are concerned, attending to the internal alarm clock and getting on with things may mean that you make amends to others. It may mean that you choose to do things differently the next time.

But if you allow the alarm clock to go on ringing, in the form of feeling ongoing guilt over a long period of time, your nerves will be jangled in the process. Imagine an alarm clock ringing night and day for years! The sound of it will, quite literally, throw off your internal guidance system and throw you into ongoing distress. If the alarm clock is guilt and you fail to turn it off and get on with your life, after atoning in whatever ways are personally and socially appropriate, you will forever have a serious block to forward momentum in your life. Examine yourself, atone for your mistakes when you need to, forgive yourself, and move on.

Ask yourself:

- For what am I not forgiving myself?
- Do I need to make amends?
- Have I learned from the error?
- Do I live my life differently because of the error or do I need to make a course correction?
- What judgments do I have about myself, standing in the way of self-forgiveness that may need to be examined?

Explore all the things for which you are not forgiving yourself and examine them carefully. Act in ways that not only make amends to others where needed, but in ways that do not erode or destroy your own dignity. Then get on with your life. Let the alarm clock awaken you, shut it off, act, and move on!

For What Am I Not Forgiving Others?

Just as not forgiving yourself does internal damage—spirit damage—so does not forgiving others for their wrongs and transgressions. I am not suggesting you allow yourself to be a doormat for others, nor am I suggesting you forego personal boundaries around acceptable/not acceptable behavior from others. What I *am* suggesting is that just as you have made mistakes in this life, so have others. Sometimes those mistakes have had serious consequences. But just as you need to acknowledge and then turn off the alarm clock of guilt for yourself, you need to acknowledge and turn off the alarm clock of judgment over the slights of others.

Some things are easier to forgive than others. *I* am not going to make a judgment for you as to whether some wrong done to you in this life can or should ever be forgiven. That is for you to decide. What I *am* going to suggest is that you examine the things for which you are not forgiving others.

- For what am I not forgiving others?
- Do I need to do some clearing work about it?
- Do I need to talk with the other person(s), explain (in a way that is not hostile or otherwise punishing) my disappointment or anger, and be open to amends that can be made?
- Do I need to examine my own patterns of judgment where others are concerned?

Do you need to forgive others for residual feelings you have over slights or wrongs done against you? Turn off the alarm clock, take appropriate action, and get on with your life!

A Sense Of Relief

Once you are clear about what to take with you on your journey and what to leave behind, you may find yourself breathing a sigh of relief. Excess baggage is a burden and choosing to take the wrong things is a waste. Discovering what you need, packing that, and leaving what you do not need behind is not only smart, but it frees up an enormous amount of energy for the journey ahead. Congratulations!

Chapter 3

MARSHALING YOUR RESOURCES

*Let me suggest three wells in which
you can dip your cup…the Well of Love,
the Well of Surrender, and the Well of Nature.*

The path may disappear ahead of you, revealing no secrets about what lies in store. You must surely walk the path on your own, putting one foot in front of the other, but this does not mean that you walk the path unaided. You have already prepared for the trip and have done some preliminary outfitting, in the form of equipping yourself. You should also discover, accept, and marshal your resources. It will make each footfall along the path easier.

What do I mean by marshaling your resources? The Universe is an abundant place. *You* are an integral part of the Universe, a part of the universal whole. This means that *you* have access to the limitless abundance of the Universe and, in fact, are yourself a part of that abundance. The wealth of abundance in the Universe is a natural resource to you. If you have never thought of it in this way, let me be the first to tell you that you have an inheritance available to you, a rich inheritance that is yours. You need only open your awareness to it, acknowledge it, and claim it. Once you open yourself to the resources available to you, simply by being a member of the All That Is, you can *rally* them, that is, bring them to bear on your life and your career journey.

What are the first steps to marshaling your resources?

- Before anything else, you must invoke the primary power: Trusting the Universe. What next?
- There are three wells that will refresh, renew, and transform you: The Well of Love, The Well of Surrender, and The Well of Nature.
- Become familiar with the Medicine Wheel and the Great Spiral.
- Practice intent and flexibility.
- Make death your ally.

Trusting The Universe

It is easy in the everyday world of work to forget your connection with the Universe. The Universe has a thousand other names including God, Divine Presence, Love, Higher Self, and The Force, to name a few. It does not even matter if you are agnostic or atheist because most people, if they are honest with themselves, believe that there is a Sacred Otherness with which they are connected. If *you* do not, then this book may not be for you. Of course, you may want to read it anyway.

The worlds of work and cosmology (the nature of the Universe and our place in it) were not always seen as separate. There have been long periods within human history in which the vast realm beyond our small and immediate field of vision was seen as vibrant and alive, organic and, in fact, an organic whole. Within this view, work was not separate from spiritual and mystical experience, work was quite naturally included.

The Scientific Revolution of the Seventeenth Century turned its back on this organic and holistic view of the Universe. If a God was still considered, then that God pulled the strings of a mechanical Universe that was without animation, without soul and without purpose, but knowable to man and controllable. Man was also seen as being machine-like, capable of being manipulated and controlled. Gone were mystery, animation, and a connection with the Divine. It is impossible for me to write these words without feeling the life and soul being sucked out of the everyday life and work of the individual.

That disconnect has endured into the twenty-first century. Never mind that quantum field theory and chaos theory point to an essentially non-linear universe, composed of fields of possibility, with an inner order to what is seemingly disordered. Unfortunately, the average person's understanding of science is seriously behind the actual discoveries made in science. And our model of business, which is based on the way humankind describes the Universe and how it works, is surely light years behind our individual understanding. Many thinkers have made valiant attempts at describing a way to view work that is holistic and grounded in both the spiritual and scientific. The assimilation of these ideas into the business world, however, is in its infancy.

I am asking you to put aside, for a while, any culturally based assumptions you may have about the world of business being orderly, linear, clock-like in its precision, dispassionate, and rational. If you retain that thinking, your career exploration will be obsessed with the orderly, linear, clock-like, dispassionate and rational. While I am not suggesting that these things have no place, I *am* suggesting that to trust in them to the exclusion of a fundamental trust in the non-linear, organic and mysterious will have the effect of blocking everything the Universe is waiting, happily, to do in your service.

So, the journey has begun. You are on the path, but make no mistake; the path you are on can be one of your own making instead of one well worn by others. How will you know if it is someone else's path? If you walk a path that is not your own, you will likely be guided by what your parents or childhood teachers said you *should* want and what you *should* do, whether or not these things hold resonance for you. You will also be guided by what your spouse and/or friends *expect* of you, whether or not you expect these things of yourself. You may feel a slight sinking sensation in your solar plexus as you contemplate the judgments and expectations of others. You might even find yourself both titillated and frightened by the counter thought of an alternative possibility.

Your own path, if you choose it, may take you into exactly the same kind of work you have been doing or to work that is only slightly different. On the other hand, it may take you into completely uncharted territory. That it *is* your path will be clear because you will feel a sense of satisfaction and congruence within you, even if you are a bit afraid of exactly where the path is taking you.

For the moment, begin your journey by putting one foot in front of the other. You will be guided on the path in many ways. Begin by choosing to trust in the Universe, trust that the next paying creative engagement will come to you, and trust that your process of career exploration will be perfect for you. Choose also to see the possibilities around you with beginner's eyes, freshly, as a child sees the possibilities without fear and with a sense of wonder.

Notice that I am using the word *choose* in each of my requests of you. I am doing so because trusting and seeing the world with beginner's eyes *are* choices. I do not believe anyone is born with a greater capacity for these two things than anyone else. His Holiness The Dalai Lama may seem to do these things effortlessly, *but he has had a great deal of practice.* I have not spoken with His Holiness about this, but I suspect that when *he* faces doubt or a jaded view of the world, he is quick to make the choice to employ trust and beginner's eyes. You can do so, too. Every time you make that choice, it becomes easier. I am not going to tell you that doubt and weariness with the ways of the world will not overtake you at times. I am only asking that you begin with trust and a fresh outlook and that when you catch yourself losing those perspectives, as you will at times, choose again. Choose trust and choose freshness.

It is as simple as that, though I will not profess that it is always easy. I am reminded that Albert Einstein reportedly once stated that there is only one real question, that being whether the Universe is a friendly place or not. I am asking you to hold fast during this journey to the belief that the Universe is, after all, a friendly place.

What if the Universe really is a friendly place? What are the implications of this? If you begin to feel within yourself the overarching friendliness of the Universe, you begin to trust that the exploration of your career/life path is perfect for you, is exactly where you need to be. You have shrugged off the old and are growing into the new, as a snake sheds its old skin, as a caterpillar is transformed into a butterfly, as a flower arises in the spring, fresh and new after winter dormancy.

This is very much about giving up your claim to what has been, emptying yourself and being patiently open to what is to come. Yes, patiently open. Why? Because Divine timing is not *your* timing. Because Nature cannot be pushed. Because the plan for you must unfold.

Cindy was working in a nursing home when her daughter, Emmie, was a baby. While she had enjoyed the work, the minimum wage pay was insufficient to meet her needs as a single parent. Scanning the classified ads, Cindy had found a position that looked promising, that of manager for a company that provided weight management services. Not having yet regained her pre-pregnancy figure or weight, Cindy believed she was in a position to empathize with company clients. She imagined herself returning to her svelte former self while helping others, an appealing idea, particularly when coupled with the management level pay.

Cindy interviewed and was hired for that position quickly. Her college degree, coupled with her background in both governmental administration and retail sales management, made her an appealing candidate. Unfortunately, while she was appealing to the employer, the job proved less than appealing to Cindy.

Cindy quickly discovered that the job title was not indicative of the job duties. In fact, there were several "managers" all working at the same time. Further, the job involved telemarketing, something Cindy found repugnant. Yet, Cindy felt trapped. She could not return to her nursing home position and she hated her new job.

Cindy had been in her new position for only two weeks when she and two peers were sent out of town for training. Her peers had far more experience with the company and shared stories about their employer that horrified Cindy. More than ever, Cindy was certain she had made a big mistake in taking the job.

The training was poorly organized, poorly executed, and exhausting. Back in her hotel room that night, Cindy felt not only weary and discouraged, but also somewhat panicked about the future. Unable to sleep, she tossed and turned. *What am I going to do? I can't stay in this job and yet I have to support a baby!* Frightened, Cindy lay in bed and sobbed.

Suddenly, a light appeared in the room. The light was so brilliant that Cindy first thought she was seeing car headlights, shining into the room through the curtained windows. She arose from the bed, went to the window, and pulled the drapes aside to discern the light's source. There were no cars with their headlights on and no other apparent source for the light, yet the light still shone, brilliantly, in the room.

Years later, Cindy would say about that night, "Somehow I *knew* that I was being told not to worry, that everything would be all right. Still, I actually wanted to *argue* with that understanding!"

After a week of going to work feeling sick to her stomach because she hated her job, Cindy quit, deciding to trust the message she had been given that night in the hotel room. Soon after, she learned of an opening at a social service agency. Cindy applied, got the job, and is still with the agency, thirteen years later.

The guidance Cindy received with a flash of light, when she was anguished and desperate, proved true. Everything *did* turn out all right. And she is thankful that her initial response to the message that night was met with loving understanding by a Universe she came to realize can be trusted.

Let me be very clear. I am not stating that you begin your journey by declaring your trust in the Universe, then lazily sit back and wait for something to happen. There is no question that you must engage yourself in the process *and* trust the Universe, not simply rely upon the Universe to do all of the work for you. But I also believe that while action without trust may get you a new job, if that is what you want, it may only be the ordinary job instead of the extraordinary one, the one that is perfect for you. As with Cindy, the combination of trust, attentiveness to opportunity, and action can produce what is perfect for *you*.

So how do you go about tapping into this trust? You may be feeling a bit bruised from your career experiences thus far. You may be wondering if you can even trust your own instincts, let alone something that seems obscure and ineffable. Let me suggest three wells in which you can dip your cup, as often as necessary, to refresh you and assist you in developing trust while you are on the path. These three are: the Well of Love, the Well of Surrender, and the Well of Nature.

The Well Of Love

The Well of Love is a good place to start. There are more ways to think about love and, therefore, more ways to become stuck with it, than just about anything else I know. We love our spouse or significant other. We love our parents, children, and siblings. We love our country. Hopefully, we love ourselves. But we also may love Shakespeare and Shelly, cheesecake and crab cakes, butterflies and bluebirds, roses and radishes. In other words, what we refer to as love covers a great deal of ground. I am not going to narrow the definition. Instead, I will expand it even further and, in so doing, make it as simple as possible. I am defining love as everything that reflects the highest within us, everything that calls forth compassion and good will, everything that resonates with warmth and light, everything that is spacious, strong and open.

What is the opposite of love, by this definition? It is that which is closed and small within. It is that which grasps and that which harbors envy, jealousy and greed. In other words, the opposite of love is fear. Fear does not inspire trust. In fact, fear feeds on doubt and mistrust.

Trusting the Universe has everything to do with developing love for yourself and expanding that love to encompass everyone and everything. Loving yourself includes learning to be gentle and compassionate with yourself, just as you would be gentle and compassionate with a small child. Fear has a way of materializing often and in surprising ways. When you find it in yourself, it is appropriate to acknowledge it. *Oh, there you are again, my fear*. It may also be appropriate to spend time examining and facing the thoughts and feelings behind the fear, and then choosing again, this time choosing love. Accepting yourself as human, as sometimes given to fear, as being the complex being you are, makes it easier to accept these same conditions in others.

Proof that drinking at the Well of Love refreshes and instills trust in the Universe is found in the very practice of loving. Catch yourself in the act. How do you feel? Exactly! The next time you find yourself having just been cut off by another car in heavy traffic, catch yourself feeling anger (one of fear's many forms) and choose again. Send out a blessing to the person and check how you feel. You are in a long line at the grocery store, it is not moving, and you have a tight schedule? Radiate white light from your heart outward to encompass the other people in line: the checker, the bagger and, ultimately, everyone in the store. Again, check how you feel.

Choosing love is so nourishing it can become a habit that borders on addiction. The most amazing things can begin to happen when you choose love. You will probably notice that people begin to respond to you more positively and, even when they do not, you are less bothered by it. You may find that synchronicity increases in your life. You may even find that things with which you have been struggling begin to fall into place. Trusting the Universe becomes easier because you begin to feel that the Universe just may be on your side.

Between jobs, I found myself restless. I was happy to have left the job, but impatient about finding my next creative engagement. I had begun to wonder if I were as good at my profession as I had assumed. A few companies had shown an interest in me and I had even had several interviews. Like the proverbial bridesmaid, I had been a finalist more than once, but never the chosen candidate. And like that proverbial bridesmaid, I had begun to wonder if I would ever be chosen. I was beyond remembering that it was not just a company that did the choosing, that I had a voice in the matter, too. I just wanted some company to see my value and offer me a job.

In my restlessness, I had begun to close myself off to others, and even to myself. I became moody. I lost interest in pursuing leads and I lost the inner spark that had made me a loving and caring person. I was afraid that the "between time" would become protracted and the lack of income would cause financial problems. The fear fed upon itself and grew larger. The simple pleasure I took in nature lost its luster.

Then a friend who lived in New Mexico, just south of Santa Fe, invited me for a visit. A spirited and spiritual person, I had missed Raven since her move from Colorado. I put aside my concerns that I would be less than an entertaining guest and accepted her invitation. In a part of the country where *every* route is a scenic route, I took the *most* scenic route I could find, highway 285, all the way from Denver to Santa Fe.

We had a good visit, cooked and ate wonderful food, hiked, went to the Indian Market, and enjoyed one another's company. Her friendship and love for me began to rekindle my own love.

The day I left, I decided to take a detour on my way back to Denver. Raven had suggested I stop in Chimayo, a small town north of Espanola. There was an old mission church there she thought I would enjoy. I had no expectations, only the desire to extend the renewed sense of well being I felt. I found the town and the church effortlessly.

The church was simple and unassuming. I walked up to it and, as my right foot crossed the threshold, I felt a total body tingling, starting at my feet and working its way up to the top of my head, like the movement of kundalini through the body. Once inside, I stepped into the chapel and took a seat near the back. I sat and prayed the prayers of one often confused and too frequently desperate. Then, after a time, I stepped out of the chapel and into a small room that contained an earth filled well professed to have healing qualities. I collected a small amount of the earth, left the room, passed a row of crutches left by those who had been cured in this place, and went outside.

But something in me felt I was not finished. I circled around to the front of the building and re-entered. Once again in the chapel, this time I chose a seat near the front. I sat and mentally said, *Okay, I'll shut up now. I'm ready to listen.*

What happened next was the strongest and clearest voice from the Divine I have ever heard. Loud, loving and firm, in my mind came the words, *Love is the most important thing!* I sat quietly, aghast at the power of it. After a time, I left the church to continue my travels. Suddenly, I was taking a different trip.

> Back at home, those words returned to me, repeatedly. On a daily basis, I made a conscious choice to love. My sense of self returned. My caring for others returned. My interest in the natural world returned. I was back! The next creative engagement did not come quickly, but the rest of the journey to it became infinitely more enjoyable.

The Well Of Surrender

The Well of Surrender is the second well that will refresh you as you journey. Surrender can be challenging for those of you who, like me, have had many years of practicing the fine art of control. We are legion. Many people who have grown up in dysfunctional homes become attached to control because it seems to make life saner and easier. Control works in many ways. It increases a sense of personal power, is active, makes you feel productive, and frequently gets results. For those of you who have worked long and hard to gain a measure of control over your lives, please understand that I do not suggest you now simply abandon what you have gained. Consider, however, that there is a place beyond control where new gains can be made through surrender.

Surrender to what or to whom, you may wonder? This is not about surrendering your will to a guru or your life to a cause. It is about surrendering yourself to the possibility that beyond what you can perceive through your five senses, beyond what is provable, and beyond the known may be a place of infinite knowledge, compassion, and wisdom.

Consider for a moment that you have a Higher Self and that this Higher Self exists beyond the concepts of space and time. It is eternal and is linked with the Larger Oneness. Its knowing extends outward in all directions and has access not only to what and who you have been, but what and who you will be and are becoming. This is possible because in the Higher Self's natural realm, there is no past and future as discrete things, only the ever-present now.

What about free will and the ability to make choices? Consider your

Higher Self as the internal part of you that provides a gentle nudge based on a larger knowledge of who you are and why you are here. Choice and destiny need not be mutually exclusive in the realm of the Higher Self. Both are operative.

Within this context, the Well of Surrender is that place, deep within, you go to for guidance from the Higher Self. You need but breathe deeply and relax your normal grasp on ordinary reality to welcome this guidance. Surrender involves a willingness to tap into the eternal, that which will move you towards choices that are consistent with your highest good. Surrender involves a deep understanding that, as a human, enfleshed in the body you have chosen for this life, your five senses reveal only traces of the eternal. Surrender is an invitation to the Higher Self to show you what is possible, to lead you to what will nourish you and further the development of your soul.

The act of surrendering often begins with a profound sense of the present. You suddenly find yourself right here, right now. The past and the future are held suspended because you realize you can do nothing about the past and the future is unknown to you. In that sweet moment of grounding yourself in the present, you give up control because you are struck with the simple and profound fact that control is a mirage. You surrender to the power of the present and with it, you surrender to an understanding, deep in your being, that you are not in charge *anyway*.

Start simply. Start in the present. When you catch yourself thinking about the past or future, mindfully choose to bring yourself back to the present: this fork I am washing; this letter I am creating on the computer; this pet I am caring for; this flower I am planting; this breath passing in and out of my body; this warmth of sun on my skin; these birds singing around me. Pull yourself into the present and, almost immediately, everything around you becomes visibly brighter and more in focus, beautiful, and alive.

There is a sense of openness in the present for it is in the present that you can begin to feel the power of the possible. An understanding, perhaps dim at first, may begin to overtake you. You realize that when you cease to struggle, you can begin to feel connected with everything around you and can begin to tap into the flow of the Universe. The voice of the Higher Self begins to speak because you have suspended struggle and grasping; you have invited the Voice of Eternity to speak to you.

The Well of Surrender is also connected with how you relate to the possibilities within the ever-present now. Begin by moving through life with an over-arching sense of love (the Well of Love). With that sense of love, realize you can have only what you choose for yourself and this act of choosing happens at a deep, not a surface, level. Welcome the guidance of your Higher Self to align your choices with your higher purpose. Set your intent. Move through the world with thoughts, feelings and actions that support your intent. Then surrender.

It is a sometimes frustrating truth, but a truth, nonetheless, that the more you obsess on what you desire, the more you repel its manifestation. Just as you need to pause and take a deep breath to hear the voice of your Higher Self, the Universe seems to need a pause and a deep breath from you to manifest your intent. Grasping does not work and what is obsession if not a kind of frantic grasping? It does not work because it implies that you do not trust the Universe to provide, you do not really expect that your heart's desire will become manifest. Grasping does not work, also, because it tends to push for limits to the timing and form of the manifestation. If you would manifest your deepest desire, the highest version of outcome for your highest self, then you must relinquish being too specific. The Universe, in its ability to distill down your deepest intent, has the amazing ability to provide your deepest desires.

Think of it this way:

> A young woman wants to further her career. She has been working as Director of Human Resources in the not-for-profit sector. The social service agency at which she currently works has undergone several changes in management and severe cutbacks in funding. It is time to move on, and she

believes her best chance is to look at the job market with other not-for-profits because that is where much of her experience has been.

She begins a search, networking with everyone she knows, surfing the Internet, scanning the classifieds in the Sunday paper, and unearthing every not-for-profit in the state. She completely ignores the for-profit sector because she cannot envision herself finding a suitable job there. She sends out dozens of résumés and has several interviews. Nothing comes of it. She cannot seem to find a position that satisfies her desire to contribute at a strategic level, work for a cause she finds compelling, or fulfills her need to use her skills fully in a fast-paced environment. Every organization she talks to seems to be bureaucratic, stodgy, and more interested in their human resource department pushing paper than connecting people with the vision of the organization.

Not five miles from her home is a small, high-technology startup that is growing rapidly and has come to the conclusion that the one-person, administratively oriented human resource department they currently have is insufficient to meet their growing needs. They need someone with vision, brains, a strategic mind, and the ability to creatively address the human resource needs of a company that is going to triple in size over the next two years. Their leading edge product is a sophisticated piece of software that can be used by the blind. An understanding of not only the complexities of human resources, but also the complexities of the systems in which their product might be used is something that the company would like to see in their Director of Human Resources.

This *could* be an exciting career move for our dissatisfied Human Resource Director in search of a new career opportunity, but it is not available to her. She is not looking for it because she is blind to the possibility, not having stepped back to look at the for-profit sector. She has not left room for the possibility that something greater than her vision may be out there.

You *may* eventually have what you obsess about, but if you insist on that very thing, circumstance or person, what you get may not be as grand or perfect for you as what would manifest if you looked to your deeper longings, set your intent on them, and surrendered both the form and timing of manifestation to the Universe. True, if you obsess, you may end up with a crude representation of what you desired, but manifesting even that may take a protracted period of time because the act of obsessing is like pouring molasses into the workings of the Universe.

Surrender, in the form of *releasing the expectation of any particular outcome,* is a very good way to enter the flow that will manifest your heart's desire. You are more likely to hit the target of your deepest desires when you surrender your archer's arm to the perfect aim of the Universe. **Love provides the energetic fuel and surrender provides directionality.**

I began this book by writing an essay, then another essay, in response to an inner need to write and, in particular, an inner need to write about career and job search. I started in a safe, conservative way. I was not at all sure the world was ready for what I might say, so I made sure that what I said was not too telling about me or my approach and did not stretch too far beyond the limits of conventionality. I was not particularly inspired after the first few essays and had a great deal in my life to distract me from writing, so I put the writing aside.

When I returned to the writing, much time had passed. My perspective had changed, birthed of new understandings. I began to surrender to the book itself and to what the book wanted written. I set about writing with new zeal and with the firm intent to produce the kind of book on career exploration and job search that did not currently exist among the plethora of writings on the subject. I continued to be somewhat cautious, not wanting to risk losing readers who shy away from the metaphysical.

I wrote in a way that spoke to what was missing from the guidance typically offered on the subject of careers, addressing what I thought of as Universal Principles. But I also wrote in a way that continued to be safe to the part of me that did not want to risk revealing too much of who and what I was, let alone the extent to which I *really* thought the Universe works in relation to career.

I quickly found myself stuck, despite the fact that I felt I had more than enough material for a book on the subject. I could not move forward and what I had already written seemed to be missing something, like a soup missing some essential seasoning.

More time passed. During that period, I found that my internal gyroscope had found a new balance after a period of intense change and personal transformation. I found myself surrendering, more frequently, to the voice of my own spirit. I found myself increasingly conscious of the guidance around me and increasingly willing to both *believe* that guidance and *do* what I was guided to do, despite how skeptical I might be and despite the risk to my sense of public persona.

During this period, a name came to me in a vision. I soon discovered, through a rather magical series of events, the name to be that of a recording artist, famous in particular circles, though previously unknown to me. Once I had personal experience with some of that artist's work, I e-mailed him to thank him for the music I found personally inspiring and uplifting. Somewhere in that e-mail, I referred to the calling that had led me to shamanic work.

What followed was a series of e-mails between us I can now look back upon with humor, but which I found puzzling at the time. The performing artist seemed angry, skeptical, provocative—all of which seemed centered around the concept of my doing shamanic work. Seven e-mails passed between us in the space of a couple of days. As I strove to be honest and struggled to be clear, his responses became increasingly combative. At the apex of this mystifying e-mail exchange, I realized I was not only feeling chastised by someone who did not know me, but I was also attempting to soften his view of me through my response. My behavior struck me as not quite so honest or clear, after all. There was an eerie sense of *déjà vu* to it. I realized, with a start, that it was similar to my attempt to write about Universal Principles without risking offending or being too controversial.

Once I caught myself in this act of cowardice, I summarized, in a long e-mail message, what I viewed to be my shamanic worldview. I sighed deeply as I hit the send button, thinking that at least I was surrendering to speaking from my own truth, at least I was surrendering to revealing my true self.

I eventually met the recording artist and we made peace with one another. I continue to value his work and continue to be in contact with him. But something changed for me the day I gathered the courage to reveal my true self and what changed had, in many ways, little or nothing to do with *him*. It was surrendering to owning who and what I am that was important. That simple act of surrender let loose something in me I have not been able to corral again, nor would I want to.

Once I made that act of surrender, the book began to take on a new

> quality. I no longer held back in the writing, but wrote without concern for how my words, and my approach, would be taken. My job was to surrender to making the offer of my message, not to package it in a way I hoped would be safe.

Surrender is not something you have the opportunity to do only once, but many times, and at deeper and deeper levels. Drink at the Well of Surrender often and deeply.

The Well Of Nature

The Well of Nature is intertwined with surrender. Nature is *about* surrender, in many ways. Forget for a moment about the recent (past few hundreds of years, at most) tendency to whip nature into submission, and think in terms of nature as it is, apart from the concept of Manifest Destiny and apart from our mindless fiddling with it.

The sun rises and sets, the moon moves through phases on a regular basis, deciduous trees sprout new leaves in the spring, raccoons mate and produce offspring, and all of it happens without our direct involvement and, seemingly, without mindful control and effort on the part of nature. Is it not humbling to contemplate that the natural world does not require our control? There is an innate understanding in the natural world that the Universe can be trusted, an understanding that we humans either were not born with, or which we promptly forgot.

I am not anthropomorphizing. On the contrary, one of the biggest mistakes we make as humans, in my opinion, is to behave with arrogant anthropocentrism. We see ourselves as central fixtures in the Universe and everything around us is, by that definition, peripheral. Once we pull ourselves out of that fixation, we have the opportunity to experience the pleasure of sensing that we are beings made of the same stuff as everything else, neither more nor less sacred than everything else. With that perspective, trusting the Universe becomes easier, and there is nothing like nature to help us find that perspective.

While we humans have succeeded in advancing technologically over the past few hundred years, it could be argued that we have not only done so at the expense of Mother Earth, but have also failed to keep pace spiritually with our technological advances. It could even be argued that we have regressed spiritually, proportional to our dishonoring of Mother Earth and all that she holds lovingly in her embrace. If we see ourselves as apart from this incessant fiddling with nature, apart from the egotistical anthropocentrism, apart from the dishonoring of Mother Earth...then we are not accepting responsibility for the human race to which each of us belongs.

The farther we get from the natural origins of things, the farther removed we are from the natural world, the harder it is to trust the Universe, which is the essence of the natural. At the beginning of the 21st century, western civilization is full of people who are removed, in a real and substantial way, from the natural world.

What do I mean when I refer to being removed from the natural world? I mean that not only are there fewer people than in the past who either grow or hunt their food, but there seem to be fewer and fewer people who even *prepare* their own food, beginning with buying fresh ingredients and ending with the hand preparation of those natural ingredients. Many people begin the day with a bagel purchased at a bagel shop and have a fast food lunch of burgers and fries. They finish the day with food that is so over-processed and camouflaged (found in bags and boxes in grocery stores and mini-markets), they would have to give real thought to what constituted the natural origins of the ingredients, and that is assuming there is much in the way of natural origins *in* the food in the first place.

I mean that because life and the natural world can be messy and time consuming, some people: choose to fill their homes and businesses with fake plants and fake materials instead of real ones; choose to experience the great outdoors through a television travel show or nature documentary instead of spending time outdoors; feel they must have a prop of some kind, like a golf club or pair of skis, in order to enjoy their time out-doors; cannot identify an American Robin or maple leaf, even when they have robins and maple trees in abundance where they live. People spend more time in front of monitors, of various kinds, than they spend *consciously* experiencing the natural world with their five senses.

We tend not to honor or value that to which we do not give our time. We tend to devalue that to which we pay little attention. If *use it* or *lose it* is a valid aphorism, then we are at risk of losing our ability to trust the Universe because we have neglected our simplest and most grounded connection to it—nature.

I suggest spending time outdoors, hiking the hills, walking the desert, rambling through the forests, or padding along the seashore near your home. If you live in the middle of a city, find a park or take a drive into the country. Drink at the Well of Nature. Watch the trees outside your window as they change with the seasons. Allow the birds, squirrels, and other wildlife around you to advise you. Plant a flower in a pot or plant a whole garden.

Whatever form you choose, spend *regular* time in nature and spend that time mindfully, behaving as if everything in the natural world has some guidance or lesson for you, because it does. Spend some of that time without props (bicycles, skis, golf clubs, books, garden tools, or anything else that stands between you and the pure experience of nature itself), alone or with others who are willing to experience the human silence necessary to hearing the hum of the natural world.

While you are at it, become mindful about the lives of all living things. This means choosing to honor life instead of thoughtlessly taking lives. In Colorado, where I live, we are sometimes inundated in the spring and early summer with miller moths. I have been known to assist the twenty or thirty in my house at one time by returning them to their out-door homes. My husband has suggested that there is a revolving door at work, that the same moths I return to nature find their way back indoors and that there may be, in fact, no more than twenty or thirty months in our little corner of the Universe. He says I just keep dancing with those twenty or thirty.

Maybe so, but I have found that by taking care not to harm creatures who do me no real harm, I become more at one with everything, more loving to humans, more accepting of myself, and more trusting of my own place in the Universe.

The more grounded you become in the natural world, the more you drink at the Well of Nature, the more you will find effortless solutions to life's problems and challenges, including those related to your career. You will find synchronicities that lead you to opportunities, as if magically. You will discover a sense of peace with the journey and a sense of joy in where it takes you.

Gary was facing a major life decision. Having come to no clear conclusion, he decided to go camping with a friend. One clear, crisp morning, Gary set off on his own to think. He found himself following a stream that snaked its way through forest and meadow and he eventually came to a beautiful place where the stream forked, becoming two streams. This seemed a good place to take a break and Gary came to rest there.

Sitting on a rock, Gary meditated, becoming entrained with the flow of the water. Journeying within, he traveled with the stream into both forks, exploring the unknown with both innocence and openness. As he journeyed, Gary became one with the stream, the sun, the rocks, and the grass.

Later, Gary would say that hours must have passed because his return to the grassy bank was fueled by a gnawing sense of hunger. On his return to camp, Gary felt a sense of peace. Somehow, he had made his decision. In fact, it did not even feel like a decision, but a natural sense of the pathway in front of him.

That decision led, a year later, to his life-long partner, his wife, Marie.

Reflecting on that experience, so many years in the past, Gary says, "For me, being in nature is the key ingredient in my journey towards enlightenment. No plan, no wonderful books to read, no one else, just *being*, in nature, at one with the essence of life."

The Medicine Wheel And The Great Spiral

The medicine wheel can be a powerful resource and ally as you walk the path. The term *medicine wheel* is most often linked with Native American tradition, but the concept embedded in the image is found within many traditions around the world, over a long span of time. The medicine wheel symbolizes the great journey of life and its ever-changing movement. It also symbolizes the possibilities inherent in every moment, regardless of where we are on that great wheel.

Differing traditions associate differing attributes to the directions on the medicine wheel, sometimes causing confusion. At the end of the day, it may be more important for you to find your own meaning in the wheel than to become attached to the meanings suggested by others. That said, it might also be useful to understand at least one model for the wheel as a place to begin your own reflections on it.

The medicine wheel may be imaged or drawn with the cardinal points placed as they would be on a map. In other words, North resides at the top of the circle when facing it, East lies to the right, South resides at the bottom of the circle, and West lies to the left. This is a two-dimensional approach to the wheel, but know also that the wheel is placed within the context of *above* and *below*. You may wish to view the space above as Father Sun and the space below as Mother Earth, or simply as sky and land. You may also wish to place yourself at the center of the wheel, able to access it all and able to walk its circumference.

Attributes and qualities can be associated with the cardinal directions on the wheel. The East may be viewed as the place from whence the sun rises, a place of freshness, a place of innocence, and a place of new beginnings and spiritual awakenings. It may also be viewed as the spring of the year and, in relation to the phases of the moon, as the time of the new moon. The South may be viewed as midday, a time of great activity in the world. It is the summer of the year and the waxing phase of the moon. The West is the time of manifestation, of gathering in the fruits of labor, the time of evening. It is also the fall of the year and the ripeness of the full moon. The North represents the night, the time of withdrawing and pulling in, allowing what will awaken later to gather strength, power and wisdom underground, as a seed resting beneath the earth in winter. It may be viewed as the winter of the year and the waning phase of the moon.

Above and below all, Father Sun and Mother Earth reside. Father Sun may be viewed as the higher forces at work, our own higher consciousness, and the spiritual realm. Mother Earth may be viewed as the primal, earthly forces, our subconscious, and the richness of what is not yet manifest from which we draw to manifest in the world. Father Sun and Mother Earth are connected by a pillar of light, an energy rod of great strength, from which energy flows between them.

To view our lives within the context of the medicine wheel is to acknowledge that there is and always will be change, a flowing nature to this change, and cycles both within and without. The moon does not always wax, nor is it always full. It also wanes and expresses the emptiness of its new phase. As humans, we often behave as if we are meant to ripen and swell, to be full and to harvest our fullness, without the corresponding pulling back and within of our resources, and without the slow unfolding of ourselves. The tides, which are guided by moon, do not ceaselessly *come in*. In fact, there would be no concept of the tides coming in without the corresponding knowledge that as they come in, so they must go out. Interestingly, when the tide goes out, one can often gather many wonderful things left behind on the shore with its passing.

It may be useful, then, to place yourself on this great wheel and open yourself to walking it. The time of the East is the glorious time of the new, the time of birth, a time of powerful creativity. As you walk towards the South, you begin to feel the burgeoning of activity, the time of great growth, a time of *doing* in the world. As you continue around the wheel, towards the West, you sense the ripening towards the fullness of your adulthood, the growing potential for reaping what you have sown.

Moving towards the North, you feel that instant of wisdom and knowing that comes with advanced age along with the physical decline that is its companion. If you rest for a moment in the North, you can feel death and dissolution, and you can sense the ember buried deep within the ashes, the seed beneath the hard, cold earth. Continuing to move, now towards the East, you feel the stirrings of new life within. Finally, you return to the East, the place where you began.

You do not, of course, stop there. Instead, you continue to make your way around the wheel. Your way is neither flat nor repetitive. Father Sun and Mother Earth are always present to make your way more than a circular one, a way that follows a great and powerful spiral. To the extent that you can see your path as a spiral, it becomes both more grounded in Mother Earth and more capable of reaching upward to Father Sun. Rather than being repetitive, the spiral revisits all parts of the cycle of life in an ongoing upward motion. There is no fear of the time of the waning moon and no boasting at the time of harvest. There is only a simple and elegant flow along the spiral path of the medicine wheel.

When viewed in this way, a new sense to the ebb and flow of life is gained. Jobs—or careers—become manifest, grow, decline, and are replaced by other jobs or careers. Relationships develop, change, and sometimes even end. Fortunes may be made, lost, then made anew. Adolescent interests and concerns replace the concerns of childhood. These, in turn, give way to the interests and concerns of young adulthood, only to be replaced by the maturing interests and concerns of later adulthood and, ultimately, those of old age.

Women may have an advantage over men when it comes to understanding and living the walk around the medicine wheel, for the life of a woman is richly endowed with the ongoing movement of her monthly cycle. Many women have accessed their internal feminine nature enough to realize that the monthly cycle carries with it more power and meaning than merely the ebb and flow of the reproductive self. Such women understand that this cycle also affects the ebb and flow of the mental, emotional, spiritual and greater physical selves. It is a monthly walk around the medicine wheel, in large measure. Men can, if they are willing, learn a great deal from women about the way of the medicine wheel because of this connection to the monthly cycle.

Placing yourself on the medicine wheel, opening yourself to the inevitability of it, and consciously walking its path is, in and of itself, an act of power. It is simultaneously an act of surrendering to the greater forces of life and an act of consciously harnessing and riding them. Give yourself the great resource of understanding and using the medicine wheel and the great spiral of life as you walk your path.

Questions To Ponder
About The Medicine Wheel And Great Spiral Of Life

- Where do I stand on the medicine wheel, at this moment, as it relates to my career?
- What fears and what opportunities are associated with my present place on the wheel?
- Do I stand at one place on the medicine wheel in relation to some aspects of my life and at another place regarding other aspects of my life? If so, how can I use this to the greatest advantage, not only for me, but also for those close to me?
- What colors, animals, and symbols do I associate with the cardinal points on the medicine wheel, as well as the *above* and *below*?
- What colors, animals, and symbols do I associate with my Self as I navigate the wheel, particularly as they relate to my career path?
- What stories and events from my personal life give meaning to the concept of the Great Spiral?
- How can I best assist, nurture and support myself as I walk the medicine wheel path?
- What markers might I see along the way?

Angela had worked as a counselor in a social service agency for seven years. She was good at what she did, had forged solid work relationships with her peers, had the respect of her boss, and had received many heart-felt thank you notes from former clients. She liked her job, but sometimes felt constrained by the standard methodologies she was expected to employ, sanctioned by the parent organization. For several years, she had maintained a private counseling practice, in addition to her full-time position with the agency. She used that practice as a kind of laboratory in which to express the full range of her talents and gifts as a counselor, including her bent towards transpersonal psychology, an approach not sanctioned in her agency job.

Angela found this private practice work increasingly rewarding, both personally and financially, but she had approached that work as an activity to feed her sense of professional fulfillment rather than as a vocational focus, in part because of the demands of her full-time job. The full-time job held the attraction of providing a regular paycheck. Angela was reluctant to give up the relative security of that regular paycheck, even though she knew her private practice had the potential for providing her with an income that met or exceeded it.

One evening, as Angela curled up in bed to meditate after a particularly long and frustrating day at the agency, she found herself, deep in an altered state of consciousness, standing in a clearing, surrounded by a perfect circle of grandfather trees. The trees bent inward, providing a canopy that allowed but a thin sliver of light to enter. Though only a sliver, the light was brilliant and Angela saw herself standing in it, facing west. Beneath her feet, the earth was softened by mossy undergrowth. The trees that surrounded her, leaning in towards her, seemed to invite her to listen to the murmuring of their leaves.

Angela walked to the august tree to her left, put her hand on its massive trunk, as if touching its heart, and bent towards it, listening with the kind of soft ears that is to hearing what a gently unfocused state is to the sense of sight. The grandfather tree reminded her of all that she had done in the seven years she had worked for the agency and of the professional maturity this work had provided her, allowing her to feel grounded enough in traditional practices to test out new and more creative methods in her private practice, methods that were more consistent with her personal spiritual bent.

Called next by the venerable tree standing to the north, Angela approached this ancient one, placed her hand upon its trunk, and again listened with soft ears. This grandfather tree spoke to her of what was needed at this time in her life. He encouraged her to be grateful for all the abundance she had received through her position as counselor at the social service agency. He told her that while both she and the agency had benefited from the working relationship, it was now time for her to release the agency and move on. It had served its purpose. Angela felt an instant of fear, which was quickly replaced by acceptance of the truth of this grandfather's words.

Angela now felt coaxed by the tree to the east to approach it. As she walked from the tree that stood in the north to that which stood in the east, she felt as the goddess Inanna during her visit to the Underworld, stripped of both clothing and flesh, then made anew. By the time she reached the luminous tree of the east, she felt reborn to a new professional self. The tree of the east spoke to her of new beginnings, of approaching her private practice as a full-time venture, of adding to that some time writing and teaching. Angela felt inspired by the images that the tree invoked in her.

Finally, Angela was drawn to the tree that sat in the south. She eagerly approached this old but virile tree. As before, she placed her hand on its trunk. This time, she felt the renewed vigor that would accompany her change from agency employee to self-employment. She saw the work that would be involved, but knew her soul would be so nurtured by the work that it would frequently feel more like play than work.

Angela left the tree of the south and returned to the center of the clearing. She raised her arms high overhead and called out gratitude to the guidance that had brought her to this place. She reached down and caressed the earth, again offering gratitude, this time for the grounding that Mother Earth had given her. Next, she bowed to each of the grandfather trees that had offered their counsel, sending each her love. Finally, she turned her attention inward and, as she did so, she found herself stretched out on her bed, her awareness returning to the room around her.

Angela arose from her meditation with a sense of herself and what she could do with her life such as she had not felt in a very long time.

Intent And Flexibility

Two powerful allies and resources on the journey can be found in fully marshaling your intent and flexibility. As mentioned earlier, surrender should be accompanied by intent. Another way of viewing and approaching this is to consider how intent and flexibility, seeming polar opposites, are entwined in one of the great paradoxes of life. Your intent is both the fixed point of your effort and the act of making effort itself. Intent involves your ability to focus on what you want, identify your place in the world, and claim it. In career exploration and job search, your intent is deeply involved in your answers to the following questions: *Where now? Doing what? Under what circumstances? How and in what way?*

If you are working with a career coach, you have undoubtedly been challenged to define the bull's-eye of your particular target. It is extremely helpful to examine where your skills lie and where they do not, what inspires and impassions you as opposed to what depletes and bores you, what and where your boundaries are, what kind of people you would choose to include in your work life as well as those you would just as soon avoid, and how you can best use your talents. If you have not already done so, I strongly suggest you apply all your learnings in this process to the task of articulating what your ideal job looks, sounds, feels, smells, and tastes like. The purpose in these activities is to assist you in honing your intent.

A career exploration journey without intent is like a ship cruising in circles. It may be a distraction, or even fun for a while, but eventually it becomes boring and gets you nowhere. The object of your intent is the destination of your cruise and your intent is the engine that powers the ship. Using the bull's-eye/target metaphor referred to earlier, the object of your intent is the center of the target, the bull's-eye, and your intent is the precision of the arm that guides the arrow towards it. Without intent, you have nothing on which to focus and no way of knowing if—and when—

you have reached your destination. The process of your career exploration/job search may be the path itself, but your intent is like a compass guiding you along the way.

If you are unsure of where you wish this journey to take you and what you wish to be doing at its destination, the suggestion that you must have intent is likely to be frustrating. Do not despair. Many a career seeker has eventually found himself at a great destination even though his intent was less than focused at the beginning of the search. In fact, a little confusion and even a little chaos can be good because it can mean you are questioning your assumptions and your life. It is important to avoid setting an intent before its time, just as it is important to avoid the wine you have just bottled before it has had the opportunity to age a bit. It is also important to gain *some* sense of intent before you incapacitate yourself through questioning and fear, just as it is important to break open that bottle of wine before it has deteriorated into vinegar.

The keys are flexibility and the knowledge that you may make a choice today and remain free to choose again at any time. If you are not completely sure of your intent, spend some time refining it through an exploration involving thinking, feeling and listening to the longings of your soul. If you are still unsure, after having made a fair go at it (say, more than ten minutes and less than ten months), then craft your intent from what you know and feel *now*. You will need a sense of intent for focus and you will want the freedom to further refine, or even totally change, your intent later. The point is to create intent and give it your commitment, as you live it in the ever-present now.

I am not encouraging equivocation or lack of discipline. Know that you will arrive at no destination if you cannot decide whether you are setting off for South America or Africa, Iceland or Antarctica, Europe or Asia, Fiji or Florida. But you *will* arrive at your destination if you spend the time to look at maps and travel books, pick a destination that speaks to you, and accept that you may choose to make some mid-course changes along the way.

Flexibility is important not only because you need the freedom to hone your vision and change your mind, but also because without it you may find a perfectly acceptable destination for yourself while missing the one that would have left you breathless with awe and changed for all time. If you are completely certain about every detail of the object of your intent, with no room for factoring in the wisdom and help of the Universe, then you may very well get the job you envisioned while missing the opportunity of a lifetime.

Therefore, develop and hone your intent while practicing flexibility.

Setting Your Intent

1. Imagine *setting your intent* as you would set a clock to the correct time. The full, positive force of your intent is at twelve o'clock (midnight or noon, whichever feels right). Set your intent to this position.
2. On a regular basis (whatever feels often enough without feeling obsessive), review your intent.
3. Has your intent moved from the twelve o'clock position? If so, is it because your ideal has changed? If this is the case, return to the *My Ideal Job* exercise. If not, reset your intent to the twelve o'clock position.
4. Take a moment to capture the feeling of your intent in its full power, at the twelve o'clock position.

Examining And Experiencing Flexibility

1. Find a time when you will be undisturbed. Sit quietly, in a relaxed state.
2. Review your life for examples of flexibility, times when it was appropriate to be flexible and you demonstrated your ability to act with grace and flexibility.
3. Review your life for examples of inflexibility, times when it was appropriate to be flexible but you demonstrated a resistance and/or inability to be flexible.

4. Examine your internal environment within each of the above circumstances. What within you allowed for flexibility when you demonstrated it and what within you prevented or hampered flexibility when you struggled with it? Make note of any new learnings about yourself.
5. Remaining alert, relax further. Enter your own internal environment of appropriate and powerful flexibility. Allow all your senses to come into play in experiencing this part of yourself.
6. Resting, alert and powerful within your sense of personal flexibility, take this sense with you to a time in the future when it may be difficult for you to be appropriately flexible. Feel yourself graceful and flexible in this circumstance. Allow yourself to feel grounded in the experience, comfortable, and at peace with yourself.
7. Return to the present, continuing to sit quietly and in a relaxed state. Going inside, ask yourself if there are simple things you can do to enhance your ability to be appropriately flexible. Can you, for instance, occasionally change the order in which you conduct your daily routine? Can you drive to work or other places you frequent by a route that is new or unusual for you? Can you select a different brand of toothpaste? Can you try a food you have heretofore avoided?
8. Whatever you can find to practice in a new or different way, commit to the practice.

Making Death Your Ally

Death is a subject that many would prefer to avoid. We honor birth, we idolize youth, we seek ways to *enliven* our daily existence, we distract ourselves with activity or inactivity, and we do everything we can to delay even contemplating the fact that death is inevitable. We are comfortable with cheating death and we have a million ways to do it. We participate in extreme sports, we eat everything our intellect tells us is unhealthy, we smoke, we drink to excess, we find the time to watch television but do not find the time to exercise our bodies, we drive without wearing our seat belts, and we ignore signs of dis-ease in our bodies. All these things have one thing in common: they are ways we thumb our individual and collective noses at death.

Even our penchant for watching movies and television shows full of violence and death is a means of ignoring death. To be sure, it is a paradox. We put death on a screen, enacted by no one we know personally, and by doing so not only make it palatable, but attempt to convince our subconscious minds that it has nothing to do with us.

But death has everything to do with us. From the moment of birth, we are on a death march. Death is unpredictable and it is this unpredictability that allows us to delude ourselves into thinking we can avoid it. Even for those who can, in some measure, predict their death, such as those with terminable illness, denial is a part of the classical response to the news. But life is terminable for all of us and we can either ignore that fact or use it to our advantage.

How *do* you use the inevitability of death to your advantage? You do it by remembering that life is ephemeral and that death may come at any moment; and in that remembering, you begin to behave as if every moment had significance because it may be your last.

Most of us behave as if we have all the time in the world when, in fact, our time may be up at any moment. This posture of pretending that we have an unlimited amount of time has the effect of trivializing the moment. We put things off and the primary thing we put off is living our lives as if they mattered. We have very little tolerance in our society for delayed gratification, but if we examine exactly what we refuse to delay, it is seldom what nourishes the soul and, most typically, it is among the myriad of things that supports us in distracting ourselves.

To use the inevitability of death to your advantage, you must make death your ally. This means keeping it nearby, perhaps behind your left shoulder as it is sometimes imaged. It means living each moment as if it were your last. It means refusing to delay that which is important to whatever is highest within you. It means examining what you do and how you do it for real significance, and then making some choices.

One of the choices you may find yourself making when you make death your ally is the choice to give less importance to what *the world* thinks and more importance to what *you* think. This choice is deceptively simple because most of us have adopted the thinking and values of some subset of the world around us to such a great degree that we can no longer be clear about exactly what *we* think and value. To some degree, that is what socialization is about. But the choice to rely on your *own* sense of what is good and right and true for *you* is a choice that is guaranteed to change your life. It may change your life in subtle but fundamental ways that are not apparent to anyone else; it may change your life in ways that are flamboyantly obvious to those around you. But it *will* change your life.

Making death your ally as you re-examine your career or pursue a job search involves examining who you are and what you want for yourself, and then *doing* something about it. You may find that you choose nothing very different from what you have done in the past. But then, you may also startle yourself with what you really want.

I am not suggesting that you ignore family obligations or community responsibility. I am not suggesting egocentric self-indulgence. I am suggesting that you honor yourself at least as much as you honor family and community, and that you make a choice to live your life in a manner meaningful to *you*, not merely live it in a way that is understood and valued by *others*.

When you make the choice to live life meaningfully, to live life as if any moment might be your last, you begin to live within your own body. You become more genuine, more graceful in your interactions with the world, and more engaged with life. You may find that your senses are heightened. You will surely find that the way you use time changes. Focus and intent may come easier and you are likely to find yourself behaving, in shamanic terms, with enhanced *impeccability*. The path you take on your career/job search journey will either stay the same or it will change, but regardless, it will take on a new quality of freshness.

A Deathbed Experience To Assist You
In Making Death Your Ally
(Also Found On Accompanying CD)

1. Visualize yourself on your deathbed. Those closest to you ask what you would like your obituary to say and how you would like your headstone carved. What are your answers?

2. From the same deathbed perspective, what would you say were your greatest achievements in life? What do you regret *not* spending more time doing? What do regret having spent *so much* time doing?

3. How do you view the work you have done, in relation to the rest of your life, from your deathbed view of the world? Is this view satisfying? Do you have any regrets?

4. What is left for you to do? What is left that you would very much like to have done but which you will be unable to accomplish because you are about to die?

5. Return to normal awareness, fully aware of everything you have learned from this process.

Tom had not given much thought to death. At 45, he still considered himself young. Death was a long way off. Even so, he enjoyed reminding himself just how alive he was. He was an expert level snowboarder, played lacrosse aggressively, pumped iron in the gym at least a couple of times a week, and climbed mountains on several continents.

At work, Tom prided himself on having a true sense of urgency in his role as IT Manager at a high technology, leading edge, pre-IPO company that was all about the need for speed. He averaged twelve-hour workdays, but it was common for him to respond to middle of the night and weekend emergencies that not only disturbed his sleep and disrupted weekend plans, but also piled work hours on top of an already heavy work schedule. Nonetheless, Tom was satisfied with his life.

Then Tom was diagnosed with prostrate cancer, the problem discovered initially during a regularly scheduled physical exam. He was afraid and incredulous. Was not prostate cancer an old man's disease? Apparently, it was not *only* an old man's disease. Was he not in good physical condition? Apparently, cancer was no respecter of buff bodies. How could he be saddled with this problem when he was so busy at work? Life suddenly appeared to be messy and without concern for his schedule. Could the cancer kill him? Yes, the cancer could kill him.

Tom dealt with the problem swiftly and decisively. He had surgery and, less than two months after the initial diagnosis, he found himself recovering at home. He was uncomfortable and out of sorts. It seemed that his whole life had come crashing down around him, even though his surgeon was confident that they had removed all the cancer. He did not feel well enough to work from his bed, although he made some minor attempts to do just that. He had not read a book in so long that the very idea seemed foreign to him. He was sure he would rather suffocate himself with his bed pillow than watch daytime television.

In this state, Tom began to reflect on his life. What had he done in his life that would live after him if he died? What was he doing with his life, for that matter, that made dying untimely? Could the company do without him? Did the buff body matter? Tom's recovery did not take long, just long enough for him to mentally replay most of the events of his life, contemplate his successes and failures, reflect on his values, re-examine his goals, and make some plans for the future.

Tom no longer felt he was bullet proof; he *knew* he wasn't bullet proof, in fact. The sense of urgency for which he prided himself was now applied to determining what would make his life of value to himself, what would make him feel his life had been worthwhile should he have a reoccurrence of the cancer...or be hit by a truck his next trip outside the house. By the time he returned to work, Tom had made some decisions.

Within six months of his surgery for prostate cancer, Tom changed jobs and changed the focus of his leisure activities. Wanting to be *off* the high tech, pre-IPO treadmill and *on* a not-for-profit creative engagement, Tom took a job with a not-for-profit agency he felt proud to call his employer and whose work he felt made a difference in the world. He even managed to make this change, miraculously he thought, without taking a cut in salary. The hours were more reasonable and the people with whom he worked seemed more interested in their contribution than in their potential for making a killing in the stock market and retiring young. He also became a ski instructor in a program for disabled skiers. Most importantly, Tom began to hold sacred every moment of every day.

"There *are* no bad days," he was known to say, "as long as you're alive to take another breath." Sometimes others saw Tom turn his head slightly upward and to his left, as if listening to someone speaking to him, over his left shoulder.

Tom learned, the hard way, to make death his ally. You need not experience a life threatening illness or event, though, to live as if this day might be your last. After all, it just might be.

It Is Your Journey
But You Need Not Make The Trip Alone

No one but you can travel the life journey that is yours, but when you trust the Universe, you are joined by a companion that is resourceful, understanding, wise, resilient, and impeccably clear about the route—your own Higher Self. As you marshal your resources, you are harnessing the personal power to live a most beautiful dream. Allow love to fuel your journey and surrender to give it direction. Allow nature to help you maintain your focus on the present moment and remind you of what is real. Make death your ally in order to keep your focus on the important. Allow intent and flexibility to provide focus coupled with options. And walk the medicine wheel of your dream knowing that the beautiful dream is one that flows along a spiral path.

Chapter 4

WHEN THE DESTINATION IS UNCLEAR

When the spirit of a person begins to move,
there is a point when time seems suspended.

ou have prepared for the journey and have marshaled your resources. A seasoned traveler and quite fond of some of the places you have visited, you contemplate journeying again to one of your favorites, the south of France. You have been to Provence so many times, you feel comfortable there, at home. The geography and the people are familiar to you. It would be an easy choice to make. But something in you longs for a new place. Peru? Australia? You are unsure. In fact, the more you think about it, the less sure you are of where you want this journey to take you. You acknowledge your longing to travel to a new place, but you wonder if you are prepared to go to a place with which you are completely unfamiliar. Do you have the resources? Will they accept you somewhere new? And if you *did* journey to a new place, where would it be?

To complicate matters, even when you *think* you know where you are going, you understand that you may end up somewhere else entirely.

There is a story told by men who worked in the Ogden, Utah rail yards during the 1940s, 50s and 60s. Hoboes would sometimes hop southbound freight trains in Ogden, intending an easy ride to Salt Lake City. Those with this intent were unaware that the southbound train was not destined for Salt Lake City, but Sacramento, California. While it began its journey

---

heading south, the train soon made a turn to the west.

During the warmer months of the year, these hoboes would be without jacket or coat. After all, they were expecting the brief journey to Salt Lake City, only forty or so miles away, where the temperature was roughly equivalent to that of Ogden. They were not expecting a long ride, passing through the Great Salt Lake Desert, which was bitterly cold at night, even in summer.

At its destination, the rail yards in Sacramento, California, those hoboes who had made the error of assuming their destination was Salt Lake City would be found dead, lost to exposure.

Even after you have committed to your transport mode of choice and think you know where you are going, you may be surprised to find that your journey can take you to a destination completely different from the one you had intended!

Many people who have spent a number of years in a particular profession, or who have held numerous jobs in the same industry, come to a point in their career journey where they are quite clear where they have been, but are less sure of where they wish to go next.

- A man has worked as a Sales Representative in the high technology arena and has been successful at it, exceeding sales quotas by 25% each year for the past five years. He feels unfulfilled and wants to do something else, but does not know what that something else might be.
- A woman has worked in the field of human resources in a manufacturing setting. She has expertise, over fifteen years, in virtually every area of human resources. She longs for a challenge and is bored in her work. She is frequently awakened in the night by a recurring dream in which she is forced out of her current job and, after a period of panic, has an epiphany or sorts, beginning again in a new career. Each time she awakens from the dream she is unable to recall just what the new career is.

Knowing you need to move on from the work you have been doing but *not knowing* to what and where is a frustrating experience. There is good news in this frustration. When the spirit of a person begins to move, there is a point when time seems suspended. This period of suspended time comes between the nascent feeling of movement and an ultimate sense of clarity about the next step. It is as if there were an internal farmer turning the soil to plant a new crop, one who, once finished with the preparation, then pauses to consider what to plant next. The farmer who plants a different crop improves the condition of his field. The person who surrenders to the deep longing to move on in her career improves the condition of *her* field too. The only difference is that her field is the field of possibilities.

How do you move from the place of not knowing to a sense of which path to take? How do you encourage the internal sage within you, that part of you which knows what will be perfect for you, to share that information with the conscious self? There is neither a single answer nor a right answer to these questions, but you are not helpless. There are many ways to tease out an answer from your own internal knowing…or at least to get closer to an answer.

Who Are You?

Return to a question asked earlier in this book: Who are you? Stripped of your roles, who are you? That is, without the job title or company affiliation, who are you? Without the title of mother/father, husband/wife, skier, runner, or golfer, who are you? Without ethnicity or race, without a socio-economic label, and without your social biography, who are you? Without classifications of any kind, *who are you?*

For many people, it is disconcerting and uncomfortable to face these questions. We sink into our roles as a way of defining ourselves, and in making this definition, we lose part of ourselves. But once you have stripped away your roles, accepting yourself just as you are, you can begin to look at yourself with fresh eyes. Introduce yourself to your Self. From this perspective, ask some questions and allow the answers to present themselves:

- What do you value in life and how have you lived your values?
- When you were ten years old, what did you want to do when you grew up and what was there about it that was so compelling? What about at fifteen? At twenty?
- What are the most compelling stories about your life? Speak them aloud or take the time to write them out. Is there a common theme or themes to them?
- What stories about others, heroes or heroines, have fascinated you most in your life? Is there a common theme or themes to them?
- What are the top ten things that give you fulfillment in life?
- In those moments when you have been *in the flow*, or *in the zone*—absolutely jazzed—what were you feeling and what were you doing?
- How do the answers to these questions inform you about where your journey may next take you?

What Do You Do When You Are Not Working?

With what do you fill your life when you are not working? Yes, you may have family/friend obligations. Yes, you must attend to your bodily needs: sleep, nourishment, and all the rest. But when you have a moment of time, what pulls on you? When you are free to do exactly what you wish, what is it that you do?

Do you have an avocation, something you love to do, with or without pay attached to it? Avocations are frequently postcards from the Universe, sent to nudge us toward our life's work, or at least the next opportunity. If you devoted yourself to that avocation, might it blossom into a full-blown occupation? What would you need to do to manifest that possibility?

What volunteer activities command your passion and time? Notice that I use the word *passion* here. The volunteer activity undertaken from a sense of obligation, without passion, will not serve you as a possible vocation. It must be compelling. It must inspire passion in you.

During my years of human resource work in corporate America, I was occasionally approached by someone in job search wanting to network, pick the brain of someone who had done extensive hiring, or get help with a résumé revision. I was open to providing this assistance, knowing that many people had been generous to me while I was in job search. I wanted to give something back. I opened my address/phone book and shared contacts. I read résumés and offered suggestions for their improvement. I served up bits of universal wisdom, as one might serve up a helping of pasta Alfredo.

In time, a local executive associated with a professional organization began to refer job seekers to me. These were senior level executives who were either already in transition or about to enter the transitional state between one job and another. I never rejected one of these opportunities. If I had a telephone message from the business acquaintance who sent these seekers my way, it was the first one I returned, regardless of how many return calls I needed to make. Not only did the job seekers benefit from our meetings, but I benefited as well. I felt enlivened by the help I offered.

Later, after I had left a position as Director of Human Resources for a computer software/service company, I began to be enticed by a possibility. What if I took the work I loved, the work with job seekers, to a new level? Was there a business in it? Some part of me doubted that I could or should make a living doing something I loved to do. Another part of me, nudged on by the voice of my spirit, gave me a challenge. Why *shouldn't* I make my living doing what I loved to do? I did an internal check and my body gave me a resounding *Yes!* I founded my business, Dragonheart. My business now encompasses much more than job search coaching, but its core still rests in that kernel of possibility: *What if I made my living doing what I love to do?*

Is There A Common Thread To Everything You Have Done?

Go to the résumé in your head or on paper. Regardless how homogeneous or heterogeneous the experience is, look behind the experience, as one might look past the characters, setting, and plot of a piece of fiction to its *theme.* Is there a common thread linking all of the things you have done? Is there more than one common thread?

Sometimes it is obvious. For instance, you may look at your résumé and see that you have been an account manager for a provider of software used in the travel industry. You have also been a free-lance writer whose articles on exotic world locations have been published in a wide variety of magazines. In one very demanding job for a manufacturing company, you were a sales representative in Europe, logging enough frequent flyer miles to take you around the world and back in first class. Perhaps you also worked for the Peace Corps in your youth. It is not much of a stretch to see the common thread of travel, specifically international travel.

It may not be this easy to tease out that common thread. Dig. Is there a theme to your experience? Is there a connection to: the outdoors; marketing; a particular field of endeavor; the arts; the sciences; a type of product; a kind of service; manufacturing; bleeding edge technology; charitable organizations; the helping professions; the media, in all its forms; the persuasion of others, from sales to politics to the ministry, or; anything else?

While the *form* the work may take can vary over the course of time represented on a résumé, it is typical for a certain *proclivity* to reveal itself beneath the surface. Sometimes it is this proclivity for a kind of activity, setting, or form of service that propels us onward, not the exact form of the work. When this is the case, you may need only turn your attention a few degrees in any direction to discern what career avenue to explore next.

> Howard had a long career in police work, culminating in the position of Chief of Police for a small Colorado town. When the headaches of being a Chief became greater than the rewards, he left police work. For a year, he taught at the police academy of a local college, then took a position as Director of Security for a school district. After a few years, he was ready to move on again. He signed up, as an independent contractor, for a company that contracted with the US government to provide services overseas. For the next year, he trained police officers in Kosovo. The conditions were

harsh, but the work was the most rewarding of his career.

After the stint in Kosovo, as he pondered what to do next, Howard looked back over his career and determined that the common thread among all the things he had done, the thing that motivated him, was *service*, especially to people and groups victimized in some way. He was not sure what work lay before him, but it was likely he would once again find a way to be of service where justice and protection of others were lacking.

To What Does Your Spirit Call You?

In his seminal book, *Ways of Enspiriting*[7], Warren Ziegler introduces a practice he calls Deep Listening™. This practice can assist anyone in accessing the call of spirit within. While Deep Listening™ can be done with another, it involves three things when done solo:

1. Become *silence*. When you become *silent*, you quiet the body and mind. When you become *silence*, you not only quiet the body and mind, but also gently *empty* an internal space, and so make space for the voice of spirit to enter. *Tip: After quieting the body and mind, you may find that it facilitates the process of emptying to allow the roles you have taken on in life to softly drop away. You may also find it helpful to gently shed the opinions/judgments you hold about yourself and your social biography.*

2. Invite in spirit. This is not a matter of forcing, cajoling, beseeching, or threatening. Spirit is invited to enter the space and speak. *Tip: As you mentally make your invitation, be authentic in expression; be true to your own voice. This is not the time to lapse into a poor imitation of whoever you imagine to be more spiritual than you. You have a spirit. You are as full of spirit as the next person. Your spirit wants the invitation in your own way, offered humbly and genuinely.*

3. Give attention. Stay open and gently focused on being silence. Give attention to whatever sensations and thoughts come to you. *Tip: Do not discount subtle thoughts, feelings, or sensations of any kind. What is*

real and true frequently whispers instead of shouts. On the other hand, also be prepared for the possibility that spirit may make its presence known loudly, blindingly, with a whole-body chill, or in some other forceful way.

Your spirit knows what calls to you at a deep level and is willing to talk with you about that calling, but you must be willing to listen. If it has been some time since you went inside and invited your spirit to speak to you, or if your spirit has frequently knocked on the door of your consciousness to no avail, be patient. Your spirit may question the genuineness of your intent to empty, open, invite, attend and listen but will ultimately accept your intent. This is your spirit, after all.

You may wish to enter into this process with one or more questions about your career and/or career exploration process placed in your intent:

- *What might now be an appropriate expression of my life's work?*
- *What work calls to me in a profound and compelling way?*
- *What, spirit of mine, would you have me be and do next?*
- *How might I live the expression of my highest calling?*

It is also appropriate to enter into this process with no questions at all, just a willingness to listen:

- *Spirit of mine, I am willing to cease the questioning and all internal chatter, to become an empty vessel. I am ready to listen.*

How Do The People In Your Life See You?

Sometimes the people who are close to you can see what you cannot. To some extent, it is a matter of objectivity. It can be difficult to see yourself clearly when you sit in your own skin. But it is more than that. Those close to you may have the uncanny ability to see the *next* version of you before you can see it or step into it yourself. This is the version you have yet to grow into, the one you may be unconsciously dancing around because some part of you is afraid.

On the other hand, those close to you sometimes become stuck in a previous version of you, one you are long past. Have you ever had lunch with someone you have been close to but have not seen for some time and found that person relating to you according to the patterns of behavior that were once you, but no longer are? You may sense that this person does not see you. You may sense that your words do not quite register. The person may seem distracted or bored and not fully present to you. She has defined you and kept that definition static, while *you* have changed. She really *is not* seeing or hearing you, at least not the present version of you.

There are also those who see you, quite clearly, as you are in the present. This can be extremely useful, but if you are at a point of confusion and restlessness in your life, what they will reflect back to you may be confusion and restlessness. They may also look meaningfully into your eyes, pat your hand, and tell you they know everything will work out *just fine*. It will be well intentioned, but it is not particularly useful.

Because any of these scenarios is possible, because those close to you may see the next version of you, one from the past, or a rather muddled present version, it is important to choose carefully whom you will probe for glimpses into yourself. It is also important to remind yourself that *you* will need to discern from what they offer that which may be useful.

How do you probe your friends in a way that will elicit useful information? Possible questions include:

- How would you describe me to someone who has never met me?
- What qualities in me, both positive and negative, differentiate me from others?
- What do you see as my biggest untapped potential?
- What do you see as my biggest blocks to fulfilling this potential?
- What am I blind to in myself that, if I could see it, might make all the difference?
- If you could wave a magic wand and place me in a profession or field of work that is perfect for me, what would it be?
- What do you believe are my greatest technical strengths? Weaknesses?
- What do you believe are my greatest behavioral strengths? Weaknesses?

- What are the most important work contributions you have witnessed/experienced from me?
- What would you like to see more of in me?
- What would you like to see less of in me?

Questions like these can inspire surprising feedback. You must be able to take a deep breath, empty yourself of judgment, and open both your mind and heart to the answers. Those close to you will only be as honest with you as you are capable of receiving that honesty with a grateful heart and thoughtful mind.

Give attention to the manner in which you ask and arrange for this feedback. It is important that those close to you know that you have opened your heart and mind to the feedback they have for you. Anyone who has been lured into being *completely honest* with another only to have the person requesting the honesty seize up, turn red, and hyperventilate will be cautious about giving this kind of feedback. Make it safe for them. Listen to the feedback with that same posture of Deep Listening™ described in the previous section.

What Is Your Internal Guidance System Telling You?

Information is offered by the Universe in many ways, not the least of which are: dreams, visions, and intuitions; the seemingly random activities of the natural world; spirit guides and power animals; synchronicities and; the immense field of what is potential but unmanifest. If you have ever solved a knotty work problem effortlessly while focusing on your morning run or have had a flash of inspiration while in the shower, you have tapped into a part of the richness of information offered by the Universe.

Some people find access to this guidance to be second nature, whether or not they are conscious of it. Look around you. Who do you know who seems to have good luck drop into her lap on a regular basis? Whose life and career seems to be charmed? Who seems nearly always to be in a state of grace? But for many, accessing the richness of the guidance offered by the Universe is *not* second nature. Some become stuck in their mental functioning, engulfed in the world of the rational, stripped of their innate faculty for attending to the magic that sits right next to them, waiting for an invitation to make itself known.

How do you regain the birthright of your internal guidance system? How do you begin to open yourself to the magic around you? What follows are but a few possibilities.

- Allow yourself to become sensitive to what is pre-verbal. Before the act, before the thought, what flirts with or begs for your attention? In many ways, this is another form of Deep Listening™, an unstructured form of it. When you quiet the mind but keep your physical senses alert, the world around you will frequently give you clues.

Pamela wonders how she can bring more financial abundance into her life. Since she left her last job, her bank balance has dwindled in an alarming fashion. She feels that something stands between her and the manifestation of new opportunities, but has no idea what it might be.

She sits on her deck, eyes closed. She empties her mind of concerns and allows the question of the blockage to drift away from her. When she opens her eyes, some minutes later, she allows her vision to be softly unfocused. She notices the grill at the far end of the deck and the dying maple tree beyond it, in the yard. They seem to be the only things in focus. Nothing else around her has her attention. Suddenly, without bidding, what comes into her mind is that she must burn that which is dead in her life.

In that moment, Pamela understands that her question has been answered. The blockage is the undone deed of burning what is dead in her life. She sits quietly, not understanding quite what this means. What soon comes to mind are memories of relationships ended and parts of herself left behind as she has changed. She also begins to see, in her mind, a parade of things in her life that no longer represent who she is: the dinnerware from a marriage ended some years before, clothing she no longer feels comfortable in, books read and never revisited, and household clutter.

> Pamela resolves to rid herself of the things in her life that no longer add value. She decides to gather them up and offer them to charity. Then she will write the names of those gone from her life, the qualities no longer representative of her, and list the things she has given away. She will have a burning ceremony and offer the energy of these things, dead to her, to be recycled by the Universe.

- Attend to the synchronicities in your life. You get up one morning thinking of a former colleague, someone with whom you have not talked for some time. You leave the house to run errands, forgetting the cell phone, and find a message from that colleague on your answering machine when you return. If you are attending to synchronicities, you will pick up the phone and call that person before putting away the dry cleaning, washing the vegetables from the grocers, or starting a load of laundry. You will put everything on hold until you have returned that call.

> Paul was attempting to network into a company he had been keeping an eye on for a very long time. The company, a business travel management service, had a great product, a strong management team, and a strategic plan that had seen it through more than one economic downturn.
>
> One day, as he was surfing the Internet, his attention was drawn to something offered by his Internet service provider, a service that linked people to their high school graduating classes. Without really understanding why, Paul visited the site and registered himself with the service.
>
> Two days later, an old high school buddy sent him an e-mail. The contact had been made through the site with which Paul had registered. Paul discovered that Steve, his high school buddy, not only lived in the same metropolitan area, but worked for the company into which Paul was trying to network. The two had a happy-hour reunion at a local pub, re-established their friendship, and quickly began to formulate a plan for networking Paul into an interview with the company.

- Pack the question about your path into your subconscious and forget about it. Allow your subconscious mind to perform the alchemical process of transforming your confusion and uncertainty into inspiration. How does this work? The subconscious will perform its magic by merging the wisdom of the unconscious realm with that of the conscious realm. The formless, non-local, contextual, and systemic soup of the unconscious marries what has form, locality, definition, and individuality in consciousness. In other words, the realm where everything is possible joins the realm where the all-possible settles into specific possibilities. Those possibilities may reveal themselves to you in the form of dreams, fantasies, visions, or moments of inspiration.

What Do You Long For And What Do You Fear?

Ask yourself what you long for. What, when you think about it, creates a visceral response not unlike feelings of love? What is so captivating it makes you stop in your tracks every time you think about it or encounter it? What, if you could do it, would you sacrifice for, as a lover would sacrifice for the beloved?

Now, what prevents you from moving towards your longing? What do you doubt about yourself? What are you unsure of in yourself? What do you fear when you allow yourself to think about what might be possible for you? What does the internal critic say to dissuade you from following your longing?

When you begin to examine longing and fear, it helps to stalk yourself. Animals of prey use all of their senses, remain acutely observant, and move with such stealth they are almost imperceptible as they track and move in on their quarry. Allow a part of yourself to be the acute observer, quiet and just a little detached, as you look for clues about your destiny and your internal roadblocks to it. Stalking yourself is akin to behaving as if you are an observer from another planet who can, somehow, see you from the outside as you go about your day and, at the same time, experience you from the inside, with all of your thoughts and emotions.

This practice requires the ability to suspend judgment. What is being observed is neither good nor bad, it simply is what it is. The inner critic must be seduced by the sheer fascination with the observation.

In suspending judgment and becoming the unattached observer, you can begin to gain access to what moves within you, stimulates your sense of longing, and prevents you from pursuing that longing. You allow the thoughts and feelings of longing and fear to come into your attention, observe them, and learn from them. Once you have done this, you can choose to act on what you have learned.

Have You Sought Answers Through Guided Imagery?

Sometimes the answers to life's questions, including those involving career, are ready to emerge into consciousness and require only a little gentle probing. Guided imagery can be helpful at these times.

You already have an internal Board of Directors. This Board is comprised of your internal wisdom: the combination of life experience, intuition, and guidance from the Universe. Sometimes it is helpful to take the direct route to it, that is, have a *meeting* with your internal Board of Directors.

Guided Imagery, Technique I
A Meeting With The Internal Board Of Directors
(Also Found On Accompanying CD)

1. Get as comfortable as you wish to be, close your eyes, and concentrate on your breathing just long enough to sink into relaxation.

2. Envision yourself stepping into an elevator that will take you from ordinary consciousness to a state of consciousness that is heightened in every way. As the elevator door closes, you notice that you are completely alone. When you look for the button pad, you see that there is only one button, the one that takes you to the top floor. You push this button and feel a delicious sense of upward movement.

3. The elevator stops and the door opens. You find yourself facing a beautiful garden of ancient trees, ferns, and flowers. The flowers, while not resembling any you have ever seen, appear familiar to you and have the surprising quality of seeming both wild and carefully cultivated. The garden flora is punctuated with extraordinary rock formations. In this one place are boulders of many different kinds of rock: clear quartz crystal, Lapis Lazuli, Malachite, Topaz, and Obsidian among them. A stream runs through the garden, singing as it rushes and plays over rocks.

4. Beyond the garden is a temple made of white marble. Wide steps lead up to the temple and there are ornate columns in front of it. The doorway leading into the temple is triangular, inspiring images of a pyramid.

5. As you step into the temple, you see twelve chairs arranged in a circle in the middle of a large, open space. There are two additional chairs in the center. Men and women of all races occupy the twelve chairs. Their ages seem to span the late teens to advanced eldership. One of the chairs in the center of the circle is occupied by a man of indeterminate age. He is mature, but nothing in his features provides a clue as to his exact age. The other chair is empty.

6. As you walk towards the group, you come to the sudden realization that you are among Masters who have gathered to give you assistance. The man in the middle of the circle stands to greet you. You enter the circle, passing between a seated man and seated woman, and join the man in the middle. He bows deeply before you in a gesture of honor and greeting. You return the bow. You look into his eyes and are overcome with a sense of complete and unconditional love from him. He holds your gaze for some time, and then motions you towards the empty chair. You sit down.

7. No one in the group speaks a word, yet you know that they are ready to join their minds and hearts in *dreaming* a solution for the questions you bring to them.

8. The thirteen bow their heads and enter into a meditative state. You

follow suit. A faint, melodic hum hangs in the air and you realize that this hum comes from the unity of Spirit among all present. You silently send your questions to the oneness into which the group has entered. And you wait, feeling a deep sense of peace and trust that the answers will come.

9. After a time, you notice that the tone of the hum in your ears changes. It is deeper and even more resonant than before. Then you begin to receive, from the mind of the group into *your* mind, the answers you seek. You have the curious experience of feeling like a computer that is downloading information of vital importance to your well being.

10. You feel an internal shift into a deeper sense of relaxation as your body incorporates the information and your mind acknowledges the rightness of it. You open your eyes and find the Masters smiling at you.

11. The Master in the middle stands and opens his arms to you. You stand and enter into his embrace, feeling blessed by the love, acceptance, and wisdom you have received from the group. You bow deeply to him, then approach the rest of the group, bowing before each as you make your way around the circle. With each bow, you send thanks from your heart, knowing that the Masters receive your gratitude with love.

12. You leave the group and exit the temple. You notice that the air around you smells sweet as you step into the garden. You cross the garden grounds and make your way back to the elevator. You enter the elevator, push the button, and find yourself blissfully swept downward. When the door opens, you enter the world from which you came, feeling renewed.

13. When you are ready, return to ordinary consciousness and allow the answers that have been given you to settle into a sense that can be understood by your everyday consciousness.

Another guided imagery that may help you on your quest for answers accesses the internal Board of Directors in a different way. Rather than being visible participants, their essence guides you as you seek out the appropriate doorway for this time in your life.

Guided Imagery, Technique II
A Visit To The Hall Of Doors
(Also Found On Accompanying CD)

1. Get as comfortable as you wish to be, close your eyes, and concentrate on your breathing just long enough to sink into relaxation.

2. Envision yourself in a beautiful natural setting, on a hiking trail that winds upward on a serious but not aggressive incline. The trail cuts through a forest of pine. The rich smells of pine and earth combine with the hum of insects and the twittering of birds to bring you into a deep sense of peace with yourself. Your leg muscles and lungs respond well to the effort of the climb and you find yourself enjoying the pure physicality of it.

3. You come to a place where the path widens out onto a mesa. You see before you an enormous rectangular structure, covering the entire mesa. It is made of rough stone and is so tall that it disappears into the clouds. You walk towards it with curiosity and note that the entire surface of the stone is covered with mysterious carvings, hieroglyphs you cannot fathom, but can sense have deep meaning to you.

4. You enter the building through a round doorway and find yourself in a long, narrow hallway that seems to stretch on indefinitely. On either side of the hallway are doors, evenly spaced, every twenty feet. You walk down the hallway, stopping here and there at a door, wondering what lies on the other side. But you are not inspired to open any of the doors. Still, you know that one of these doors opens into a room that holds the answers to your deepest questions.

5. You continue to walk down the hallway until one door calls to you. The door glows, as if for *your* eyes only. You feel such a strong sense of curiosity that you are compelled to open it.

6. You place your hand on the doorknob, turn it, and open the door. You step into a room filled with a thick, white fog that feels pleasantly cool and moist on your skin. The fog begins to dissipate and as it does, you see what this room holds for you. You realize, as you begin to explore the room, that it not only contains what is perfectly appropriate for you, but also seems to have no end to it, stretching on beyond your ability to see.

7. You take your time, exploring the room and becoming comfortable with everything you encounter within it. Finally, when you feel you have what you have come for at this time, you make your way back to the door and step out of the room, lovingly closing the door behind you, knowing you can return to this room whenever you like.

8. You make your way back down the hallway and pass out through the round door.

9. As you retrace your steps on the trail, you come to a place where there is an obstacle in front of you. This obstacle was not there when you made your way up the trail, but in a flash of understanding, you realize that it represents your fears.

10. You bow to the obstacle, thank it for showing you the manner in which you have orchestrated self-defeat, and search within for a thought, a word, or a deed that will remove the obstacle. The perfect expression comes to you. You employ it and the obstacle is magically gone.

11. You work your way to the base of the trail with a sense of your own power to manifest your dreams.

12. When you are ready, return to ordinary consciousness and allow the experience you have just had to settle into a sense that can be understood by your everyday consciousness.

In experiencing these guided imageries, you may find that they hit you right between the eyes with answers that are profound and make sense to your rational/logical mind. On the other hand, you may find that your experience is more metaphoric than rational/logical. If this is the case, dig beneath the surface and you will be rewarded with treasure.

Do You Have An External Board Of Directors?

In the previous section, I talked about consulting your *internal* Board of Directors and gave you a guided imagery to help with this process. Now I would like to extend this idea to your *external* life, the everyday reality you experience with your five senses. Corporations have Boards of Directors, why not you? There is an ancient and honored belief that wherever two or more are gathered together, there may you touch the Divine. This thought not only applies to religious practice, but also to everyday human endeavor. As it happens, two minds *may* be better than one.

In selecting possible members of a personal Board of Directors, think of those in your life who are both consistently supportive *and* consistently honest and frank with you. Those who are supportive without being honest and frank will only serve to confuse you more. In an attempt to be *nice*, they will avoid telling you when you are off track, when your latest thought is unsupportable by the evidence within and around you, when you are procrastinating, and when you are getting ahead of yourself. Those who are honest and frank with you without being supportive will fail to care for you unconditionally and will neglect the need to nurture a dream into manifestation. You need both support and honest/frank feedback.

It is also important to consider the skills the people in your life may bring to your personal Board. You *need* visionaries on your team, but you also need people who are very good at following through in practical ways, people who will nudge the vision into manifested reality. In other words, choose not only people who are good at visioning and strategizing, but also people who are good at planning and executing. You need both.

You need at least one person to serve as provocateur, that is, someone who will ask the tough questions, stimulate thought and action, stir things up, and evoke what is possible in you. This should not be a person who incites anger, nor should it be a person who is simply perverse and more interested in challenging everything than adding value. It should be someone who has a talent for either expanding the possibilities or bringing things back down into what is currently doable, whichever is needed at the moment. They have a talent for discerning what is critical to success and bring this to the surface by asking critical questions and offering thoughtful observations.

How many people do you need on your personal Board of Directors? You need enough people to provide diversity of thought and meaningful input but not so many that it is an engineering effort to manage communication and contact. That will mean different things to different people and in different circumstances. Consider the male/female balance in the group and realize that diversity of race and ethnicity can add to the group's richness.

How do you form such a group? Invite them! In my experience, humans are far more generous than we usually give them credit for being. There is an urge in the human spirit to give itself over to an honorable cause. Those who love, support, and are honest and frank with you will feel the stirrings of that urge. Be clear about the purpose of your invitation. You are seeking assistance in moving from a lack of clarity about your path to a point of clarity. You believe the experience and thoughts of others, brought to bear on the situation, can provide a breakthrough. You invite this particular person because you believe s/he has both valuable insights and the ability to work towards a common goal with a group.

Have respect for the time of those you invite. You do not wish to capture all the free time of those whose help you seek, and that assumes they even have time they consider free. Give thought to how much time you are asking of others. Put a fence around it. Ask for their participation in one or two meetings, each of a pre-determined amount of time. You may find that having a personal Board of Directors is such a valuable tool you will want this group to be an ongoing resource to you, but test out the idea with a limited time commitment. Be not only sensitive to your Board's time, but be willing to repay the gift by offering your time in service to each of them.

Does your Board of Directors need to meet as a group or can you meet with them individually? While it will require a certain amount of coordination to truly activate the power of their combined experience and thinking, you need to meet as a group. Additionally, you may want to speak individually with Board members for guidance about particular sub-issues with which they have expertise. Keep the thrust of your effort, however, on meeting as a group.

If you have not considered assembling a personal Board of Directors, it may be that you never thought yourself, your life, or your career to be *worthy* of one. I suggest that the one-person corporation that is you is completely and wholly worthy of one. The solution to your personal dilemma about where to go next on your career journey can be solved with the same combination of logical thought, group process, and intangible magic Boards of Directors use to solve business problems.

Have You Tapped Into The Realms Of Guidance And Holistic Healing?

Some of the best insights into and guidance about my life and career have come from, or been inspired by, professional practitioners of the metaphysical arts and holistic health practitioners: my astrologer, my psychic advisors, shamans, and the energy/body workers I see on a regular basis. I do not pretend that this route is for everyone and I am not suggesting you trust every practitioner without giving thought to references. But if you are open to exploring these realms, you may find assistance beyond what your rational thinking processes can provide.

My astrologer, Sally McDonald, would probably take umbrage at my view of astrology as a discipline of metaphysics. Astrology is, after all, steeped in mathematics and ancient science. What I have seen in the most brilliant applications of astrology, though, is the ability to take the potentially hundreds of hours of guidance from the data and distill it down to what I need to hear in the present moment. That ability transcends the mathematics of it. The guidance I received from my astrologer led me to my apprenticeship in shamanism and my study of energy work. My astrologer has also been one the biggest supporters of my writing because my astrological chart suggests that writing is a part of my personal path. Astrology has had a powerful influence in guiding me to what is good in my life and I continue to seek out that guidance!

Astrology can give you insights into your nature and proclivities, the vicissitudes of timing, and the planetary influences that impact your life. A good astrologer will not tell you what to do and will not behave like a fortuneteller, but will help you help yourself by working *with* the astrological forces that impact you instead of struggling *against* them.

Psychics (or intuitives, as some prefer to be called these days), the kind with references and track records, can also be helpful. Even if you have an ongoing personal relationship with guidance in whatever form it comes to you, and even when you have tapped into your internal guidance system, there can be moments when your internal vision is less than 20/20 or when you have trouble *believing* what you already know.

At those times, a gifted psychic can provide insight, support, and validation. Do some research to find one respected by both clients and peers if you have never worked with a psychic and are considering it. Check into who has a reputation for being accurate and honest. There are gifted psychics and there are charlatans. You must take responsibility for the selection process, as well as for discerning the usefulness of what you get in the interaction. Likewise, you must use discernment in determining whether or not to act based on the guidance you receive.

Shamanic work, particularly shamanic journeying, can be extremely helpful when you find yourself confused or at a crossroads in life because it is *internal* work that tends to cut to the heart of things. The journey process can be done alone, but is, in my experience, far more powerful if done through the assistance of a shaman. The shaman is trained and equipped to facilitate the journey process. S/he will create sacred space for the journey, facilitate your relaxation and shift into an altered state of consciousness, hold the energetic space for you while you journey, be your witness to the journey as you recount it, and help you make sense of it all.

In undertaking a shamanic journey, one enters an altered state of consciousness, typically through methods such as deep relaxation and drumming. The journeyer holds the intent of a question or questions about his life and travels by spirit to worlds understood by shamans all over the world as being every bit as real as the world we occupy in ordinary reality. During the journey, he may face challenges and/or receive help and guidance from spirit guides and/or power animals. Answers to questions come, sometimes in ways that are remarkably literal and sometimes in symbolic ways.

Shamanic approaches associated with Native American tradition that may be useful include sweat lodge and vision quest. The sweat lodge is a place for purification and healing and a very good place to find answers within. The vision quest is specifically designed to provide direction as to life path. If you want to explore either sweat lodge or vision quest, look for someone who is respected and considered effective by both clients and peers. Many gifted medicine women and men are found primarily through the network of those who have sought out their help and received benefit from it.

Energy/body work can be a powerful ally when you are confused about your path. This work includes modalities such as Reiki, Body Alignment, Polarity Therapy, and massage. Depending on the method, practitioner and your openness to the work, energy work can uncover and heal deep-seated mental and/or emotional wounds, provide flashes of insight, reconnect you with your spirit, connect you with the realms of guidance waiting to assist you, unblock and/or re-pattern the flow of energy in the body, release memories buried within the body's tissues, and relax you to the point of sheer bliss.

Have You Examined The Patterns In Your Life?

It would be comforting to think we act cleanly in each moment, our actions inspired by a deep understanding of our life's purpose, and our steps in the ever-present-now perfect for its fulfillment. It would be comforting and I believe it is possible, but to realize this possibility, many of us need to step back and review the patterns in our lives. Too often, the patterns we have adopted, like well-worn grooves, inspire our actions in a largely subconscious way.

As I stated earlier, if you have failed to clear an emotional charge with a person or persons from your past, you may find yourself meeting that person repeatedly in work and social interactions. She will have a different face and a different name, but will trigger the same reactions in you. These repeated experiences can represent deep-seated patterns we carry within.

How do you know if a pattern or patterns may be blocking your ability to see clearly and move forward with confidence?

- You find yourself drawn to or working for/with one version or another of the same person over and over again and find the relationship less than satisfying.
- Knee-jerk reactions to reoccurring situations are the norm and not the exception for you.
- You continue to expend energy in directions that seldom produce fruitful results.
- You have a familiar and not altogether pleasant feeling associated with seemingly varied experiences. There is also a corresponding sense that there is something in common to these experiences, no matter how disparate they seem to be on the surface.

Any of these may suggest the need to consider the possibility of disruptive patterns in your life. Ask yourself what you are reminded of when you encounter the person, the knee-jerk reaction, the wasted energy, or the familiar feelings. Then accept whatever comes to mind: a time when you felt defeated, an adolescent disappointment, a childhood fear, family struggles, the death of someone important to you, a moment of embarrassment…whatever. Recall and feel the experience. Dig for more. What does *that* experience remind you of? Allow whatever begins to bubble up in your thoughts and feelings to become fully formed. Dig deeper still, if necessary. In fact, keep digging until you sense you have come to a root thought/feeling, an origin.

Once you have unearthed the origin of the pattern, you may wish to do a clearing exercise, journal your thoughts and feelings, or take some other action to exorcise the pattern that has been holding you back. It is important to also set the intent to make new choices when faced with whatever has triggered the pattern in the past.

At a time when I felt my business was not getting off the ground, I was also experiencing disappointment over relationships with business and social friends. I paused to look with fresh eyes at what was problematic about the manner in which I was relating. In doing so, I realized that in almost every case where I found something missing in or dissatisfying about a relationship, it was a relationship almost single handedly maintained by me. I was the one initiating contact. I was the one rearranging a schedule to accommodate the needs of the other. I gave gifts of personal time, effort, support, and material offerings with little or no reciprocity. I was extending myself repeatedly with little thought to the natural law of giving and receiving: *giving and receiving are equally important and where one is lacking, the hoop of life is incomplete and the Universal Principle of giving and receiving is violated.*

I asked myself what this reminded me of and began to think about my history as an employee, before I had struck out on my own. I had frequently put in unreasonably long hours that left no time for anything but the basics of eating, sleeping, and the occasional load of laundry. Not only did I work longer and harder than most of my peers, but I also worked longer and harder than most of my bosses. The result of my Herculean efforts had been more work, heaped on. I could always be counted on, after all. I wanted to be more than smart, competent, and hard working. I wanted to be seen as brilliant, indispensable, and able to take on anything. I was willing to extend myself beyond reason to fit that image. I succeeded in being described by others exactly as I wished to be seen. It did not buy me much acknowledgment where it counted, however. I had to fight for each promotion and pay increase. Most of the time, though, I told myself that my employer appreciated me, even if I saw no demonstration of it.

I began to see a pattern represented in both business/social relationships and in relationships with employers. My tendency was to work hard at both, take all responsibility for the relationship, and have no expectations of reciprocity. Again, I dug deeper and asked what I was reminded of by this.

My internal digging eventually took me to the mother lode or, more accurately, the mother/father lode. I had learned, at an early age, that it was going to be difficult to get either my father's attention or my mother's approval. I remembered dancing in front of the television at about the age of three, trying to get my father to notice me. I remembered trying to fit my mother's definition of a *good girl* in hopes of winning her approval.

My parents had not been unusually neglectful or abusive. They were ordinary people with their own patterns, arising from their own personal histories. I had loved them. I had greatly valued the time with them, as an adult, before each died. Whether or not my childhood learning was based on any objective fact, it was based on my subjective experience. I had developed a pattern of doing many things to demonstrate my worthiness of attention and approval. I could even say that this pattern had served me well in that it had played a part in my worldly success.

The pattern was now blocking my forward momentum in both business and relationships, though. It was time to break it. I worked through the pattern of origin, the one I had developed in childhood. Then I worked my way forward. I dropped many of the dysfunctional relationships, as if they were alien spawn. It was not difficult. I had been the one making most of the contact and doing most of the work. I just stopped doing those things. The friends-that-weren't dropped away effortlessly and I appreciated the relationships that remained on an entirely new level. I also vowed to only extend myself in business in ways that honored a fair exchange of energy.

My block became unblocked. I would like to report that I have this one mastered, but I have periodic lapses into the old patterns. I manage it as an alcoholic would, one day at a time.

Do You Need To Complete Your Education Or Update Your Skills?

It is easy in a world of responsibilities to forego some of the things that might truly make a difference in your life. Did you begin a college education but not finish it? Did you complete undergraduate work but put off the graduate work? Do you need new skills for this new world?

Sometimes a lack of clarity about destination is related to doors that are closed because of inadequate education or training for work that would fulfill you. We have many excuses for not getting the skills we need: too little time, too little money, enough experience to make up for the lack of education, no family support for the effort, considering ourselves too old to seriously consider it, poor study skills…and on and on.

Yet, if the issue is training, no excuse is going to provide clarity about your destination. The doors that are closed will stay closed until you get past the excuses. Ask yourself some serious questions about what you need in the way of skills to get to *any* destination that might be appealing and what it will take to get the skills. Then act. Your college credits from ten or more years ago may provide more currency towards a degree today than you think. Some colleges actually provide credit for work related experience. You may find that all you need is a refresher course or a six-week program to update your computer skills. You will not know if you simply continue to spin excuses.

What Is Your Passion?

If unseen, Divine forces guide you, does it make sense that your guidance would have you pursue something as a life path for which you have no passion? I think not. You have something to offer the world and you are probably not going to offer it with enthusiasm if you have no passion for it. The world needs passion and I believe that perfect work for anyone is work for which s/he has passion.

This does not mean that honorable work to pay the bills and support your family is neither good nor acceptable if it is work for which you have no passion. Paying the bills is a good thing. Do that. At the same time, examine where your passions lie and begin to pursue them.

Is there likely to be only one thing for which you have passion? This may be the case, but many people have passion for more than one thing and, in some cases, many things. Frequently, the task is one of either narrowing the work expression of your passions to avoid spreading yourself too thin or finding a creative way to a singular work in which many of your passions can find expression.

Is it likely that the work for which you have passion will remain constant throughout your life? Many of us know people who began to express passion for a given occupation at a very early age and have remained loyal to it. But not everyone is a Mozart and Mozart *did* die at a young age. Some people find that their passions shift with age and experience. What seemed vital, important, and exciting at twenty may no longer hold your interest at fifty. Life is a process of ongoing transformation and the work that calls you may shift with those transformations.

If your destination is unclear because your passions have transformed over the years, turn your attention from that which once held passion for you towards that for which you currently have passion. If your destination is unclear because you have attempted to ignore your passions, then begin to pay attention to them. If your destination is unclear because you are so entrenched in day-to-day life that you have not even stopped to ask yourself what you are passionate about, begin to ask that question now.

Who Do You Admire?

Who do you admire: living, dead, fictional? What, specifically, is it that you admire about them? Who are the heroes and heroines around you, the extraordinary ordinary people? What inspires you about them? The distance between what you admire in others and that which is admirable in yourself (or could be) is a very short distance. You make the leap by realizing that your heroes mirror an aspect of you. They may have that aspect perfected, while it may be nascent or underdeveloped in you, but it does reside within you.

Look at the qualities you admire in others and contemplate how they express those qualities in the world. Then excavate your personality, your character, your talents, and your skills until you find a place within that mirrors those qualities. This may seem shockingly arrogant at first, but if you pursue this practice, you will find that it is nearly impossible to admire what you do not carry within yourself. They may be only seedlings or they may be fully developed, but these qualities are within.

Perhaps you admire Warren Buffet's combination of keen business sense and down to earth personality. You may have difficulty finding the Warren Buffet within, but I urge you to look for him or, more accurately, the qualities you admire represented by him. You may also greatly admire Oprah Winfrey for her compassion, generosity, guts, and ability to relate to people from all walks of life. My guess is that Oprah will not mind at all if you embrace the Oprah Winfrey within you. Perhaps Don Quixote appeals to you because of his ability to see beyond everyday appearances to the magic of what is possible. I would suggest that there is a bit of Don Quixote within you.

Acknowledging the hero and heroine within (and each of us has both) tends to awaken heroic vision and heroic acts.

What If Money Were Not An Issue?

You can create an immense block for yourself by saddling your future to current monetary considerations. What you love and have passion for may not bring immediate fortune, but it is more likely to bring eventual fortune than that which you disdain. No passion, no juice. No juice, no gain. What if money were not an issue? What would you do? Who would you be? It is a paradox, but once you remove money from the equation, you sometimes free yourself up enough to allow money to flow to you.

Steve had the ability to bring order to chaos and focus to the obscure. His appearance was conservative, militarily ordered even, but his demeanor was so welcoming that he inspired the immediate confidence of others. Steve held a position in a good company, but it was a position that did not completely capitalize on his skills. He was a trooper and persevered until he could hardly get up in the morning. Then he quit.

Steve did his homework and worked hard: he looked at his strengths and weaknesses; he cleared everything that held a negative charge for him; he examined his passions; he allowed himself to dream; he did self-assessment, including The Birkman Method®; he developed a stellar résumé; he networked; he interviewed well; and he was completely open to synchronicity.

During a meeting with a partner of the firm he had left, Steve discovered that his quiet strength had become obvious to his former employer in his absence. The partner speculated that he could use Steve in a role supporting the CEO, a role in which Steve's administrative strengths and clear sense of structure combined with his business savvy, maturity and strategic mindset to free up the CEO for critical business development without sacrificing business acumen. The partner speculated that the firm could justify the position in, perhaps, six months.

Steve asked two critical questions: What keeps you from acting on this now? What would you do if money were not a consideration? Steve had removed the obstacle of financial consideration. The firm's partner immediately perked up and Steve could literally see the wheels turning in his brain. The partner became excited. Freeing up the CEO to do business development now instead of six months down the road could make all the difference in the firm's success. He had faith in Steve and once the time frame was blurred by Steve's simple questions, many things became possible.

The business partner went back to the drawing board. Steve was offered a position with a very modest salary, but a healthy bit of equity in the company.

It is true that not everyone has the ability to take the kind of risk Steve took, but many people have the ability to step back from their lives, make a plan that includes lifestyle simplification, and plot out a course that fulfills the soul, whether or not it fills the pocket book in the short run. The result, a few months or a few years down the road, may be financial fulfillment as well as personal fulfillment.

Have You Given Your Destination A Chance To Find You?

If your destination is a part of your destiny, then give destiny an opportunity to find you. Sometimes what we are looking for finds *us* instead of us finding *it*. Employ patience, alert awareness, openness, and faith. If your next destination is truly your destiny, you will recognize it by a certain sense of momentum that originates outside you, one that pulls you in a particular direction with the force of gravity. It may feel almost irresistible.

You may feel compelled to act in a logical way that also has a super-logical sense to it. Those actions will do harm to none and will support the energy of love.

You may have a sense of recognition when it comes to people, places, or events that feels very much like a *déjà vu* experience. There may be a sense of appropriateness, of harmony, even of being in a state of grace.

Attempting to describe the moment when a person steps into her destiny is difficult because it exists within one's ordinary life, yet has a decidedly non-ordinary quality to it. But unlike non-ordinary states in which a person has fled their mind and risks harm to herself or others, this is a state in which she steps out of her ordinary mind and into the purpose of the larger Mind.

Find A Fresh View

If none of the questions asked or suggestions offered in this chapter triggers clarity for you, then allow your own creativity to take over. Do whatever pulls you out of your ordinary perspective and gives you a fresh view. When I was a child, I sometimes climbed up on the family picnic table to stand on top. The world seemed completely different from that perspective. Change your perspective just long enough to see your personal geography in a fresh way and your destination may become clear!

Chapter 5

THE RÉSUMÉ

...the right word used in the best way
is a lovely thing.

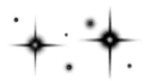

In some ways, your résumé can be likened to your passport. It validates who you are and tells where you have been. It is a brief and intimate look at you and, because of this, you may be considerably ego-involved and attached to your résumé. Almost every résumé, even the one that has been recently revised, needs revision and improvement, preferably with the help and review of your career coach and/or someone who knows your work history well. Even a perfect résumé can be improved. Because of this, your first task is to have a respectful but serious conversation with your ego about your need for an open mind and an open heart in reviewing and revising your résumé.

That done, get down to business. Before you do anything else, think about what you are trying to accomplish:

- You want to represent your experience and credentials in a way that will command the attention of the person reading your résumé *quickly* because the reader will not tarry long on it unless there is a compelling reason to do so.
- You want to represent your experience and credentials honestly, which means that you want to neither overstate nor understate them.
- You want to be known by your accomplishments, particularly those shining hours that have been important in your career.

- You want your uniqueness to come through on paper.

  The reader will want your résumé to accomplish some things, too:

- S/he will want to be able to quickly and easily determine whether to seriously consider your candidacy for a position.

- S/he will want to know where you have worked and when, without having to search for it.

- S/he will want to know, in terms easy to understand, what you have done that fits the hiring criteria.

- S/he will want to know the outcomes you have accomplished, not simply what you have spent your time doing.

- S/he will want to see dollars, percentages, numbers and other metrics.

- S/he will want to know your credentials in clear terms that include where and when you earned them.

There are as many ways to structure your résumé as there are people who are very happy to give you an opinion on the subject. Both good and bad advice await you. Take the time to explore the résumé expertise of those who would advise you, including how recent the knowledge base is from which they are drawing. What is effective and what is not changes with time. A résumé style that may have produced good results ten years ago will not necessarily produce good results today. The guidance provided in this chapter represents but one way to approach the résumé, a way that has achieved remarkable results for a good many people but, nonetheless, only one way.

What follows are suggestions for structuring your résumé.

Considerations For Structuring The Résumé

- Your résumé will be read for little more than 30 seconds, at least on first review. This means you must quickly capture the attention of the reader and tell your story in a compelling but brief way. If you succeed in doing this *and* the story you tell happens to fit the needs of the organization whose hands it has fallen into, it will get a second, more deliberate reading.

- Have clear and accurate contact information at the top of the résumé's first page. You may choose to center this information and put a border around it to enhance the appearance. It is also useful to have your name at the left hand top of the second page to ensure that this page can be reunited with the first page should they become separated.

- Consider justifying the right margin (as well as the left) on the body of the résumé. It gives the document a finished, professional look.

- In most cases, the first section should be entitled *Experience*. The exception to this *may* be the recent college graduate with little relevant experience in the field for which s/he is exploring. Note that I suggest the word *experience*, not *professional experience*, *relevant experience*, or some other phrase with a qualifier.

- Under the *Experience* section, structure the résumé in reverse chronological fashion, with the most recent experience listed first. This is particularly important if your career has been primarily in the same field or fields that represent some logical relationship to one another.

- If your career has spanned many unrelated fields, with only some of them related to the field you are now exploring, you may wish to structure the résumé in a more functional way. This approach arranges the body of the résumé in a skills oriented fashion, rather than in a reverse chronological fashion. I rarely suggest this approach. Even meandering and unconventional careers are frequently best represented in a chronological format. Functional résumés can be cumbersome for the reader. Think carefully before choosing this format.

- List the name and location of the most recent employer, justified with the left margin. On the same line, justified with the right margin, list your dates of employment with this employer. Provide years only, not months and years. For example, 1999-2001, *not* November, 1999-December, 2001. List your title with the organization, in bold, directly below the name/location of the organization.

- Double space after the title and summarize, in no more than two or three lines, who the company is. I refer to this as *framing* the company. The reasons for framing the company are two-fold. First, understand that anyone reviewing your résumé will make a mental association between you and your former employer. Whatever status the former employer has also becomes your status, at least to some degree. Make the best of it by framing the company in the best possible light. Secondly, not everyone reading your résumé may be familiar with the company. This is your chance to inform. Is it a local, regional, national, or international company? Is it a start-up or has it been in the business for 75 years? Is it a $2 million company or a $2 billion company? What is the industry? How many employees? Example: Vice President of Sales for this $20 million, 100-employee manufacturer of sports attire whose products are distributed nationally.

- Double spaced below the framing statement, bullet the position's significant components. Include outcomes and accomplishments, using metrics wherever possible. Put outcomes in bold and/or italics to draw the reader's attention to them. *The need for outcomes and metrics cannot be stressed enough.* Example: Won significant new business by redefining sales strategy/tactics and forming strategic partnerships with key distributors. **Increased sales revenues by 50% each year over a five-year period.**

- List most important, significant, and/or compelling items first.

- Use action words that have power and authority. Avoid acronyms, except when they are an accepted part of the English language, but do use industry-accepted terms and street language when they can be used to add power, add color, or make a point. Examples: Orchestrated…; Up-sell customers….; …in a guerilla market.

- Use this same format for each employer over the life of your career, or the past twenty years if a complete listing would render a résumé longer than two pages.

- A section entitled *Education* or, if appropriate, *Education and*

Certifications comes next. Unless you are newly out of school with little or no professional experience, this section should come *after* the *Experience* section.

- Under the *Education* section, list the last degree obtained first (in bold), the institution at which it was obtained, the location of that institution, and the year the degree was awarded. Justify the date with the right margin and put it in bold. Below this, list preliminary degrees in the same fashion. Put the degree (BA, BS, MBA) in bold.

- Use the same approach for listing certifications and licenses.

- If you have published books or articles that are relevant and significant, list them, providing this listing does not extend your résumé beyond two pages. Create a separate section for this entitled *Published Works*. If you prefer, simply refer to the fact that you have published books and/or articles within your field. If you have a lengthy list of published books/articles relevant to the field/position in question, create a résumé addendum for them, but do not include them in the body of the résumé.

- The same approach may be used for those with significant and relevant experience in professional speaking. A section entitled *Speaking Engagements* can follow the *Education* section. Provide the title of the speech, venue, and year in which it was given. As with publications, do not have this section on the body of the résumé if it would render a document longer than two pages. Instead, create an addendum to the résumé.

- Those in technical fields like computer science should have a section outlining technical expertise if this is relevant to the field/job being sought. This section may be entitled *Career Skills*. Career computer professionals should list the hardware, platforms, software, programming languages, and networking systems expertise they possess.

- Do remember that your résumé should be designed to differentiate you, positively, from everyone else. This is not the time to play small. In my experience, far more people under-represent than over-represent themselves on their résumés. Represent the full breadth and depth of what you have done and give yourself credit for all your accomplishments. This is the time to stand out, not blend in!

In addition to the traditional résumé, these days it is important to have an electronic/scannable résumé. This form of résumé is covered in a section further on in this chapter.

Avoid These

- As a rule, do not have a section entitled *Objective*. The reviewer will likely pass right over this section. Remember, you have 30 seconds of the reader's time. Do not waste precious résumé space on what will probably be ignored. Objectives tend to be so general and/or limiting as to be useless. Also, avoid using an *Executive Summary* section for the same reason.

- As a rule, avoid a section summarizing your major accomplishments. These are better placed within the Experience section and, if you craft that section well, your story will have better flow, be more compelling, and meet the 30 second criteria more easily than if you have a separate accomplishments section.

- As a rule, do not have a section that summarizes behavioral skills and abilities. If you have described your positions/accomplishments well, these will be obvious to the reviewer.

- As a rule, do not list the standard office equipment on which you are proficient or the standard business systems with which you are familiar. *However, as stated in the previous section, if your work is in the computer hardware/software arena, or some other high technology area where the equipment and/or systems you are familiar with and work with regularly is critical, then add a section to list these.*

- Unless you are applying for an entry level, non-skilled or semi-skilled position, do not list your high school diploma or GED. It will be assumed.

- Do not state your interests and activities. You are wasting space. If appropriate, this will naturally come up during an interview (which you are far more likely to get with a results oriented résumé).
- Do not state that references will be furnished upon request. This is assumed.
- Under no circumstances provide information about your age, marital status, or religion.
- Avoid listing training when it consists of numerous individual seminars and workshops. To do so will likely have an effect on the reader that is counter to what you intend. That is, the reader may assume that you are grasping at straws where credentials are concerned.
- Use employment dates. It can cost you consideration for a position if you fail to do so.

As one with many years experience on the *other* side of the table, as the hiring authority, I can share with you some of the things that have put résumés in the *not to be considered further* pile.

If the résumé is poorly organized, unclear, or omits important information, it will likely be given little or no consideration. For instance, it is typical for an employer to have experience requirements that include a minimum number of years of previous experience in a given area. If the résumé does not include employment dates, it is impossible to determine whether the applicant fulfills the experience requirement. Do not expect the reviewer to call you for this information.

Likewise, if the reviewer must struggle to make sense of how and why you are suitable for this position, your résumé will get little or no consideration. Submitting résumés for every position that seems appealing, whether or not you are qualified, wastes both your time and the time of the reviewer. If your experience *is* relevant, but your résumé does not make this apparent, prepare a custom résumé for this particular position.

I have also discounted résumés from professionals that were sloppily prepared, had problems with word usage, spelling or syntax, or otherwise appeared the product of someone who was lazy or lacked mental horsepower. If you are applying for a professional level position, rely neither on a thesaurus for the right word in the right place nor the most obscure word you know with the most syllables. You may come across as pretentious or pompous. Worse, yet, if you use words with which you are unfamiliar, you may appear to have a poor understanding of the English language. That said, the right word used in the best way is a lovely thing. Do not arbitrarily ratchet down your usual vocabulary for the masses.

If you are applying for a position that assumes detail orientation, such as a secretarial position, ensure that your résumé is free of errors. In fact, ensure that your résumé is free of errors regardless of the position for which you are submitting it. I have known the résumés of those applying for administrative services positions to be summarily dispatched to the résumé graveyard when they contained errors that any competent administrative services applicant should have caught. Do not rely on your computer's spelling program. Proof your résumé, have others proof it, and proof it again—in that order.

Occasionally, a résumé will be so bereft of dates that the reviewer suspects the person submitting it has something to hide, like age. I have encountered this and have worked with individuals who have been misled by well meaning coaches into omitting critical information. Many people over the age of forty are concerned they will be discriminated against based on age, despite the fact that such discrimination is patently illegal. For that reason, I will address the issue, as it relates to the résumé.

Those over forty (and especially those over fifty), take a moment to consider why an employer might discriminate against you because of age. Get very specific. Might an employer think your skills are out of date and rusty? Might an employer think you may be inflexible of mind? Might an employer think you will not have either the mental or physical stamina for the job? Whatever you conjecture might be in the mind of the employer, *this* is what you must counter on your résumé, where possible and sensible, and during the interview, when it does not make sense to address it in the résumé.

Do you fear that the employer may view your skills as out of date? If they *are*, shame on *you*. The potential employer has every right to seek the best skills for the job and you have every responsibility to ensure that you are skilled and prepared for the kind of work you desire. If you *have* kept your saw sharpened, your mind quick and your skills up to date, your résumé should reflect it, in your accomplishments and/or in your education and certifications. Do you think the potential employer may view you, because of your age, as someone lacking in creativity? Again, your creative endeavors will be represented on your résumé, at least those related to your paid employment. Do you fear the potential employer will think you lacking in stamina? If your work has required persistence, long hours and effort substantially beyond the call of duty, it will likely be reflected in your résumé or your cover letter.

Admittedly, your best shot at showing that age has seasoned and ripened you, not decimated you, may come during the interview phase of the hiring process. Admittedly, also, there is an occasional unscrupulous employer who *will* discriminate solely on the basis of age. Ask yourself if you really want to work for this employer anyway. Most employers do not care what your age is, they care what you can *do*. You can frequently dispel any concern about age before it ever arises by demonstrating your ongoing accomplishments on paper. Further, you will boost your personal energy field by refusing to submit to age-based fear!

It has been suggested to me that some employers will favor youth over maturity because the inexperienced worker commands significantly lower wages than the experienced worker. This is sometimes true, but no sane employer looks at wages without also looking at the real requirements of the job. If the job does not require extensive experience and the employer's budget will not stretch to accommodate more seasoned applicants, then the employer *will* often select the lesser skilled candidate rather than ask a more seasoned candidate to accept far less than their skills should command. That is the employer's right. In fact, the seasoned candidate may be bored by this job anyway. If you are serious about the opportunity and know that the salary offering is less than you have previously commanded, ask yourself if you are willing to take less than you have in the past. If you are, let this be known in the cover letter (*not* on the résumé) in as dignified and genuine a manner as possible.

The Electronic/Scannable Résumé

Business technology changes so quickly that I am reluctant to address the issue of electronic/scannable résumés because anything I say may be out of date by the time you read this. That said, know that at the time of this writing, many (and maybe most) people who have a traditional résumé also need an electronic/scannable one. More companies than ever before are using résumé management software. This trend, combined with the ease with which documents can be scanned, makes it critical for the job seeker to create an easily scannable résumé containing words the résumé management software will identify as pertinent and important. Further, the entire arena of Internet recruiting accentuates the need for electronically manageable résumés.

The Internet processing and/or scanning of résumés creates new requirements that fit with the current limits of this technology. Résumé management software, for instance, tends to *latch onto* nouns more than verbs. Because of this the e-résumé needs to include nouns the program is looking for, those most relevant to the position being filled. Likewise, buzzwords and industry jargon may be recognized as *key words* by this software, making it not only acceptable, but necessary, to include them on the e-résumé. Additionally, formatting may need to change significantly to make the résumé easily scannable.

Because this area of job search is changing rapidly, do some Internet research on the *current* requirements for electronic/scannable résumés. There is ample help via the Internet for you to produce an electronic/scannable résumé that will impress the potential employer every bit as much as the traditional résumé can when well thought out and well constructed.

The Employment Proposal

In the morass of information and advice about how to present yourself on paper to potential employers, it can be difficult to sort through what makes sense and what does not. Good information and advice promote honesty and get results, while faulty information and poor advice promote manipulation and/or do not get results. The problem is that while most people can detect honesty versus manipulation easily enough, the potential for results is more difficult.

One relatively new concept in the job search arena that can be both an honest approach and get results is the employment proposal. While I do not suggest the employment proposal as a replacement for the résumé, there are times when you may want to have a well-crafted résumé *and also* create a customized employment proposal.

You may want both because the two documents do two different things. The résumé is a snapshot of what you *have done* and accomplished in your career. The employment proposal is a business proposition outlining what you *propose to do* for a company. While employers typically post descriptions of the jobs for which they have openings, the employment proposal turns this concept on its ear. It describes an employer's need, a job that might benefit the employer by filling that need, the skills of the person proposing to do that job, and the benefits to the employer if they accept the proposal. In other words, rather than simply being a job ad in reverse, the employment proposal is a business plan targeted to a specific audience.

To create an employment proposal with meaning and power, you must employ focus, do your homework, and create a custom product that makes good business sense.

- You must view yourself as an entrepreneur with something enticing and different to offer.
- You must be able to target the appropriate company or companies.

- You must craft a statement that demonstrates you have done your homework and understand both how the company operates and what you can do to further its success.
- You must present yourself and what you have to offer so compellingly that the potential employer wants you on board.

The employment proposal is wasted if you mail it to the general office address or to the human resource department (unless, of course, it is an employment proposal for a human resource job). It must be targeted to the manager/executive with decision-making authority in the area you are proposing to place yourself. The employment proposal is also wasted if you cannot back up what you have so brilliantly put on paper with a sparkling interview and if you do not have the demonstrated skills to do what you are proposing.

You will still need a résumé to articulate what you have done in the past. Further, most companies still require résumés from candidates, for legal reasons. But in cases where an employment proposal makes sense, the résumé is backup and the proposal *brands* you and sells you as talent worth considering.

The employment proposal is not for everyone, nor is it appropriate in every situation, but when used in the right circumstances it can give you the *wow* factor that makes all the difference.

Just as a passport is still required for travel to exotic and foreign places, the résumé is still required to gain entrance to consideration for a job you are seeking. But just as a passport may not be sufficient for entry into certain countries, where a visa is also required, so the résumé by itself may not be sufficient to get the attention of the potential employer. You may also need a visa, in the form of a cover letter. Read on.

Chapter 6

THE COVER LETTER

...find a connection between the company and yourself.

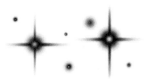

If the résumé is your passport, then the cover letter is your visa. That is, it does not attempt to apply to the world at large, but the specific *country* to which you wish to gain entry. Assume that if the reviewer will spend little time on the résumé (the thirty second rule), she is going to spend even less time on the cover letter (maybe ten seconds). Because of this, you need to craft the cover letter carefully to capture the attention and imagination of the reviewer.

Begin with the obvious. Where did you learn of the position? What is the title? The first paragraph of the cover letter should include this information in large measure to ensure that your résumé and cover letter will not get lost among the hundreds landing on the desk of the overworked administrator logging it into a system. The first paragraph should also state, in simple terms, your level of education (if it meets or exceeds the educational requirements of the position being sought) and the years of relevant experience you have to offer.

In the second paragraph, you have an opportunity to demonstrate what you know about the position and industry. Succinctly present your relevance to the organization's specific challenges and needs. If you have seen job requirements in writing, or have had them represented by someone who is knowledgeable about the position, this is the place to relate what you have to offer to their specific needs. Be careful, though. It is suicidal to present words like, "I know I have a great deal to offer your organization...," or "I know I would be a fit for your organization because..." Arrogance and mind reading will get you nowhere. Simply state your understanding of their requirements and those items from your experience that fit them.

There *is* a time for mind reading, actually, and that comes in the third paragraph. "I know that no representation of a job can adequately convey everything you are looking for, but I know that the healthcare industry [or software industry or *whatever* industry they are in] is changing rapidly. [This is true for almost every industry, but few candidates will actually admit it in a cover letter, so you will look brilliant.] What I suspect you are looking for is..." At this point, you seize the opportunity to fold in important items not in your résumé: leadership, the ability to manage and effectively orchestrate wildly divergent activities, integrity, the ability to leap tall buildings in a single bound...whatever.

The fourth paragraph should acknowledge something that few job candidates acknowledge. It is a fact of life that what *really* gets jobs is not merely excellent educational and experience qualifications, specialized skills, or a great smile but **FIT**. What is fit? Fit is the composite of behaviors and style that resonates with a particular organization.

Few candidates acknowledge the importance of fit, let alone address it. One of the ways you can command the attention of potential employers is to talk about fit openly. If, a few days after you send off your résumé, you detect a faint but audible sigh of relief in the air, it will be because whoever is reviewing your cover letter is breathing a sigh of relief that *somebody* gets it. That somebody, of course, will be you.

How do you address fit? You address it directly. "I know that fit is an important part of any hiring decision. I would welcome the opportunity to explore whether John/Janine Doe is a fit for XYZ Corporation." The reviewer will wonder if you have psychic abilities and are reading her mind. In addition, what the reviewer's brain will likely register from the sentence, on a subconscious level, is *John/Janine Doe is a fit for XYZ Corporation*. This subtle impact will only work if you use your name, not the word *I*. Otherwise, what will register in the reviewer's brain will be *I am a fit for XYZ Corporation*. They already work for the company. Psychologically reinforcing *their* fit is of no use to you!

What is left? There is little left to say beyond encouraging them to contact you if they have questions and providing your telephone number.

The format I have given assumes you have information about a real job opening. But what if you do not? What if you have done your research and have a keen desire to present yourself to a particular company without knowing whether there is a job opening in your particular area of skill and experience? The format is not much different.

First paragraph: state how you discovered the company. Did a friend speak in glowing terms about it? Do you know someone who works for the company? Did you read about it in the local newspaper or business journal? Did you discover it on the Internet?

Be compelling. It is not useful to say you are sending résumés to every software company in the four state region. That is akin to telling the wo/man you are calling for a date that you are calling up every single person in a five-mile radius, hoping to find a compatible companion. You must find a hook of some kind. Are you looking for a start-up company, one in which you can bring everything you have ever learned to bear on its development into a major world power? Then say so. Were you impressed by something you saw on their web page? Tell them what it was and why there is resonance for you.

I know someone who once looked at the web page of a nationally known company and discovered that they actually referred to God in terms that were honest but not preachy. She was so inspired she was compelled to send them her résumé for a senior level position they had open. She did not refer to God in her cover letter, but she did relate the values represented by their web page to her own values. The point is, find a connection between the company and yourself.

The remainder of the cover letter is similar to the standard version described. It is as simple as that.

Chapter 7

NETWORKING

The process of networking can be likened to molecules
bumping into one another...without end.

The N word. Eventually the subject of networking must be discussed. There is more feet dragging on this subject than any other. You are on a journey. A friend, colleague, family member or acquaintance tells you about a cunning cottage buried deep in the woods you will be exploring. The cottage is occupied by a lovely person, knowledgeable about the surrounding woods, well versed in its flora and fauna, and aware of the occasional bit of quick sand, as well as the swampy areas. You are encouraged to seek out this person, not simply for her knowledge and savvy, but also because she is simply worth knowing.

Why would you pass by the cottage, seeing the trails of smoke curling from the chimney, without stopping and knocking on the door? Perhaps the answer is that you believe you are quite capable of finding your own way. Perhaps you are shy, an introvert at heart, and do not enjoy seeking out others, particularly those you have never even met. Perhaps you think the cottage's inhabitant will be milking the cow, weeding the herb garden or otherwise so occupied that she will not welcome your knock. Maybe you do not see the value in the information she has to offer. Whatever your rationale, whatever your excuse, get over it. Get over it now; get over it permanently.

The *N* word, networking, is about humans relating with humans. It is about contacting others who may be able to offer you leads, further contacts, suggestions, and other help regarding your career. It is also about being available to others for the same purpose.

One of the paradoxes of society is that while some people behave with bravado in relation to who they are and what they can do, the part of them that is genuinely self-confident, genuinely aware of their skills and abilities, chokes when it comes to meeting new people in job search or career exploration. Maybe, in fact, it is no paradox at all. Bravado and genuine representation, swagger and true grit, do not, it would seem, exist together.

Networking is one of the most important ongoing career tools a person can have, whether that person is on a job search journey or comfortably enjoying his current creative engagement. *Enjoying and making the most* of this part of the journey is what I endeavor to awaken in you.

Who is your network, anyway? Remember that bit of homework you did earlier, the one called *The People In My Life?* These are the people in your current network. I say current because once you begin to give it some attention, your network is likely to grow exponentially. Pull out your phone/address book, your appointment book, and those little slips of paper with names/numbers you have kept without having a specific purpose in mind. Re-examine the list you created earlier, then put the list aside and come back to it twenty-four to forty-eight hours later. Your subconscious will percolate more names/contacts within that timeframe.

If you have been buried inside an organization so internally focused you seldom came up for air, let alone scheduled lunch with anyone or attended a professional meeting, and think you have no network, this exercise will prove you wrong. You *do* have a network. Unless you have been living the life of a hermit in a cave somewhere (in which case you are probably not even in job search), there is a body of people in your life that constitutes at least the skeleton of a network. A fully fleshed-out network can be developed from that skeleton.

Before you reach for the telephone or compose a memorable letter to any of these people, a philosophical and spiritual shift may need to take place. While a fair number of people in the world are certifiable extroverts, an equal number are fundamental introverts. For the introvert, speaking with family members or friends known for a very long time may come easily, but picking up the telephone to contact someone new may be anathema to his very nature.

Even for those who genuinely enjoy meeting new people or contacting acquaintances with whom they may have been out of touch for a time, the prospects of making a call that involves asking for help may be as palatable as the mythological first trial of Psyche, assigned to her by the goddess Venus, that of separating one large pile of tiny mixed seeds into separate and identifiable piles—by morning.

Whatever your comfort level with making networking calls, you need not panic, change your personality or basic nature, or schedule a lobotomy for yourself. You simply need to remind yourself of a few basic truths and behave accordingly.

A Few Basic Truths About Networking

- We are all humans.
- You have something to offer in any interaction with another person, and so do they.
- People tend to be helpful.
- Every interaction is an opportunity for networking.
- The process of networking can be likened to molecules bumping into one another.
- Guidance is all around you and synchronicity happens.

We Are All Humans

You are a divine child of the Universe, like any other. You need be no one but your genuine self. In fact, being your genuine self is what life's journey is all about.

One of the places people tend to become misdirected on their journey is that place where one human being meets another. *You* know your strengths and weaknesses. *You* know your private self, the one with tousled hair in the morning, a proclivity for old episodes of *Star Trek*, a taste for peanut butter and bananas…and all your other idiosyncrasies. Do you think you are the only human with idiosyncrasies? Do you think, at the bottom of your humanness, you are very different from other humans?

Have you become comfortable in your own skin? If not, you might want to return to the sections on *Clearing the Organization and Accepting Yourself*. If you *are*, for the most part, comfortable in your own skin, begin to ponder the possibility that who and what you are will probably be comfortable for most—not all, but most—other people, too.

Why is that? As Douglas Spotted Eagle, famous contemporary ethnic musician and master of the Native American flute, puts it: we are all five-fingered humans and, as five-fingered humans, we are all the same. There are differences in gender, ethnicity, race, religion, national origin, political leanings, occupation, socio-economic status, pass-time preferences, and many other things. But we are, first and foremost, human. As humans, we are more alike than different, at least at a universal level. When human meets human, there is a *recognition* not possible when human meets…Martian…or human meets…table. Relax into it. Enjoy it. You are human being meeting human being. It is not only understood that you have strengths, weaknesses and idiosyncratic behaviors, it is appreciated.

Cassidy took a deep breath and entered the restaurant. At the suggestion of her friend, Kacy, she had made a call to Elliott, one of Kacy's friends. Like Cassidy, Elliot had a career in marketing and like Cassidy, he also had a passion for cooking. Elliott had happily agreed to meet with her once Cassidy had told him she was looking for new opportunities in the marketing field and Kacy had given her his name. They had described themselves to each other to make recognition in a busy restaurant easier.

Now it was *show time*. Cassidy felt nervous. Her usual confidence about her abilities was gone; her usual comfort with her appearance was flagging. It was hot and her silk suit felt oppressive. Her mind was distracted by the work she had left on her desk. Kacy thought a lot of Elliott and Cassidy wanted to make a good impression.

As she stepped from the mat at the restaurant's front door to the polished wooden floor just beyond it, her stiletto-heeled pump (every bit as stylish as anything to be seen on *Sex and the City*) failed her. The floor was slick and she was anxiously looking through the crowd for anyone resembling the description Elliott had given her of himself. She slid like the stock market during a bearish run, caught by the arms of the nearest man before she could hit the floor. Red-faced she looked up at him.

"You must be Cassidy," he said.

"Are you Elliott?" she asked in surprise. "How did you know it was me?"

"Well, it wasn't the entrance," Elliott replied. "You did seem to fit the description you gave me. But you didn't tell me that dramatic first impressions were your specialty. I'll bet you disarm potential clients every time!"

Collecting herself, Cassidy regained her footing, stuck out her hand to shake his, and replied, "Elliott, it's so nice to drop in on you."

Elliott laughed; the ice was broken. Cassidy, feeling that she had already blown any chance of appearing cool and in command, relaxed into herself. Before their lunch arrived, Elliott shared two or three of his most embarrassing moments. Cassidy laughed sympathetically. Before long, they were sharing marketing strategies that had worked for them, their best contacts, and recipes for paella.

You Have Something To Offer

You have something to offer in any interaction with another person. Exactly what that is may be a mystery to you before you make the contact. It may remain a mystery long after the contact has been made. But *something* you have to offer is a gift to the other person. It may be an idea. It may be a networking contact. It may a friendly demeanor in a world that can be very unfriendly. It may simply be the energy you project. You cannot anticipate *what* offering of yours will potentially be of benefit to the other person, you cannot plan it, and you cannot second-guess it. Life is mysterious beyond our wildest imagination. You may, in a moment of insight during or after the meeting, come to realize what your offering was or you may never know, but you *do* have something to offer.

Not only do you have something to offer the other person, they have something to offer you. The interaction between you is, potentially, a lovely exchange of energy. And the Universe loves an exchange of energy.

While you may have planned a very specific purpose for the networking contact, it is wise to avoid assuming you know exactly what the contact will provide. It may surprise you. This is not to suggest that you do your networking in a purpose-less way. It is important for you to honor both your own time and the time of the people with whom you wish to meet, so it is necessary for you to be clear about who you are, why you are making the contact, and what you wish to accomplish. Just do not assume that the purpose you had in mind will be the sole point, or even the main point, of the encounter.

As Cassidy and Elliott enjoyed their lunch, the conversation turned from marketing and cooking to other things that interested and inspired them. Cassidy told Elliott about her abiding interest in and practice of meditation. Elliott, while not practiced in meditation, was interested. Cassidy gave him the outline of a simple meditation.

During this exchange, Elliott recalled that a friend of his, the CFO for a manufacturer of golf attire and an avid meditator, had called a few months earlier, stating that they would soon need a marketing guru at his company, a rapidly growing start-up. His friend was hoping Elliott could be lured from his current company. For a variety of reasons, Elliott was not so easily lured. Cassidy's mention of meditation reminded him of that discussion. He suggested she call his friend. The timing might be right and this just might be a great opportunity for her.

Cassidy and Elliott said their good-byes after lunch, each thinking that the other was an interesting and altogether remarkable person, each

---

delightfully surprised by what the other had offered, and each convinced this was someone worth having in their life.

People Tend To Be Helpful

People tend to be more helpful than we guess they will be. When asked for an idea, lead or contact, the average well-adjusted person will engage that part of himself that is interested, likes to problem solve, and enjoys helping.

Yes, the average person is *busy*. There is work to be done, both at home and at the office. There are endless e-mails to answer and phone calls to return. There often are too few hours in the day. It is easy to fear that you are going to be seen as just one more thing to do, and not one that is going to make it to the top of the pile.

That may be true, but my experience is that most people are far more helpful than we think they are going to be. Particularly if you manage to connect with them by telephone, the very fact that you are contacting them because you are asking for help and think they have something to offer will frequently snag their attention. Why? Because humans like to be needed. We like the idea that we have something to offer another.

An embarrassment to those who would like to cast humans as completely self-serving and endlessly competitive is the truth that we humans have a cooperative side to us. At some level, we must realize we are all made of the same stuff: protons, neutrons, electrons; pure energy; star stuff. We must realize that we are all in this together. Whatever the motivation, humans really do have a helpful side. Relax and know that whomever you are contacting just might be more helpful than you expected.

Cassidy picked up the telephone and dialed the number. Elliott had given her David's name and phone number, suggesting he might have an interesting opportunity and, even if he didn't, he was a man well worth knowing. Elliott had told her David was CFO of a start-up company that manufactured golf attire. She assumed he was busy. She wondered if she would reach him live, feeling that her chances of making a connection would be greater if she did. She wondered if he would be annoyed by the call and would assign her roughly the same status as the solicitor offering a service he neither wanted nor needed. She wondered if she was wasting her time. Still, Elliott had suggested she call and had assured her David was kind, interesting and a kindred spirit.

The call went through to voice mail, but David returned the call before the morning was over. He seemed delighted to have received a call from someone referred to him by Elliott. Yes, the company was about to begin the search for a marketing guru. He very much wanted to see her résumé and, with her experience, he was likely to personally walk it over to the President's office. How was Elliott? How did she know him? Ah, the Kacy connection! He had an idea or two for her, beyond the job opportunity at his company. Did she want names and numbers? She was a meditator? So was he. What was her practice?

It was not a long conversation, but Cassidy was impressed by David's generosity, kindness, and spirit. She thought about the fact that he had responded to *her* exactly as *she* would have responded to someone calling her, saying that Elliott had referred them. Amazing!

Every Interaction Is An Opportunity For Networking

Every interaction with every person you encounter is an opportunity for networking. This includes conversations at social engagements, brief exchanges with grocery store clerks and postal carriers, and chance meetings with total strangers at airports, as well as the systematic and planned career networking.

We are all networking all the time anyway. Every time you recommend a restaurant or refer someone to a good acupuncturist, what are you doing if not networking? If you begin to see networking as the natural part of human discourse it is, networking ceases to be quite so troublesome.

Once you think of networking as something possible within the context of all your interactions, you may begin to realize that having your business cards with you at all times is a good idea. If you have company business cards, great. If you do not, it is easy and inexpensive to either print a batch on your computer or, better yet, have your local print shop make them for you. Then have them with you wherever you go. It is one thing to meet someone who could be a fabulous contact and future friend; it is another thing to provide them with an easy means of getting in touch with you. Do not allow the budding networking relationship to come to a standstill, like two strangers making eye contact for a brief moment from passing cars that speed on in opposite directions. Let him know how to reach you.

> Cassidy was not expecting it. She was smelling cantaloupe at the market when she ran into Ron. Ron was her massage therapist's roommate and though they had met, they did not really know one another. As they talked over the cantaloupe, Cassidy discovered that Ron worked for a company she had just checked out on the Internet and found to be interesting. Ron did not know much about his company's marketing department, but was willing to do some checking for her. Cassidy was happy she had begun carrying her business cards with her as she handed one to Ron with a smile. Ron reciprocated. They would be in touch.

Networking Is Like Molecules Bumping Into One Another

The process of networking can be likened to molecules bumping into one another, spinning off, and bumping into yet more molecules, without end. Human systems, it would seem, are not as linear as the charts depicting the planned and predicted growth of a business organization. And, as those networking molecules bump into one another, heat is generated. Things heat up, things get juicy, and activity begets activity.

Think about one person, acting alone. That person has one set of eyes, one set of ears, one nose, one mouth, one kinesthetic system, one brain, and one nervous system. Consider what this one person can do, without the thoughts and peculiar ways of seeing the world of anyone else to mix in. Now consider what happens to anything a human being would choose to put his/her attention to when there is the added juice of two, three, four…*hundreds* of humans.

Even if you could do it alone, why would you want to? Rugged individualism? Try building a society alone. You can be rugged and you can be an individual. It is still good to include others in the process of growing your career.

Every time you speak on the telephone, e-mail, or physically meet with someone about your career/job search, ask, "Who else should I be contacting?" If that person gives you a name, ask, "Is there anyone *else* I should be contacting?" Make a point of seeking three referrals from everyone with whom you network.

What happens when you do that? The molecules start banging into one another. One contact becomes four, becomes thirteen, becomes…well, you get the idea. Each person to whom you are referred comes with a fresh set of sensory data, a fresh brain, and fresh ideas. The more people you enlist in the effort, the better your chances of spinning into the miraculous.

David has given Cassidy three names of people with whom to network. David was kind enough to propose she tell each of them that *he* suggested she call. Each of these three gave her three more people to contact and each of those three gave her another three. Cassidy's head is spinning. She has garnered several good leads and has met many people she would like to know better. Two of the leads have generated real possibilities. She has sent off résumés and has been encouraged by the people who suggested she send them. Interviews are likely. Even if nothing results in a job offer, she feels good about the new connections.

Guidance Is All Around You
And Synchronicity Happens

I have been devouring the written word since I learned to read. Books, magazines, cereal boxes, bumper stickers…anything written is vulnerable to a spontaneous feast. I have a dozen books on my nightstand at any one time, each partly read. I may be thoroughly engaged in one book on any given day, then enticed by another the next, surrendering to the craving for a new book as if I have been on a diet of meat for a week and now long for vegetables. It is not unusual for me to allow a year to pass before I have actually finished some books because of this proclivity. I surrender to the flow of the moment in my reading.

An interesting thing has happened many times because of this progressive dinner approach to my reading. I may be pondering a problem, upset by a situation, or stuck with no forward momentum on something I am doing when some book jumps off the nightstand and into my arms. Often it is a book I have ignored for some time. Sometimes it is a new book, its pages crisp and fresh, virgin territory. I will pick up the book and begin to read. Wham! Inspiration follows. The book addresses whatever has been on my mind, either directly or metaphorically. If I were unwilling to follow the flow in my reading, I would miss a great deal of inspiration.

Perhaps this happens routinely with books because I am so enamored with the written word. I *know* it happens because I am open to it. Inspiration comes to me not only through books but, literally, from everything in my life.

During the course of writing *this* book, I have received inspiration from tapes and CDs, quiet moments of contemplation, conversations with clients and friends, the birds who look at me quizzically from the deck railing, the ebb and flow of the plant life in my garden…from many, many sources. *Always* the inspiration comes when I am gently unfocussed mentally. It may come when I am in the shower, drifting up from sleep, sitting quietly, cooking, hiking the Mesa trail, or at a halt in Denver's intractable snarl of traffic. The main requirements seem to be that my mind be freed up from deliberate thoughts and that I pay attention when inspiration hits.

What I am describing may be defined as inspiration, intuitive knowing…or synchronicity. Frankly, I care not how it is defined. What *is* important to me is that I continue to be open to this gift, however it is defined.

How does this translate to the career/job search process? When you begin to explore what is possible in your career, you sit on the fine edge between one world and another. It is liminal. In shamanic terms, it is a *between time*, like the moments just before sunrise and sunset. It is a moment between one state of consciousness and another. Such moments are profoundly magical and pregnant with possibility. They are times when the veil between ordinary reality and all other realities is as thin as the wing of a moth. Because of this, our lives have the potential for guidance and inspiration from thousands of sources.

To tap into the richness of guidance and synchronicity, you need only understand that it is possible, allow yourself to find moments of nothing-special-no-specific-thoughts, and have an intuitive net ready, as if you were ready to catch a butterfly within your psychic field.

One day you may find yourself thinking of an old college friend, call them, and discover that they have information and/or contacts valuable to your career. The next day, the lyrics of a song startle you out of reverie. Some word clicks, the name of a company you just saw an article on in a newspaper. You go to the Internet, do some homework, and discover that there are possibilities at this company for you.

The only difference between those who benefit from these numinous, significant events and those who do not is that the ones who *do* expect them, attend to them, give them credence and act on them. That's it.

I was in job search and frustrated. A friend had given me with the name of a colleague some months before.

"You need to know one another," she said. "I don't know why, you just do."

Perhaps it was because her colleague worked in a field far removed from mine. Perhaps it was because his last name was that of a man I had once loved deeply and who had recently died. For whatever reason, I had failed to make the contact. But one day, as I looked through a list of potential network contacts I had not contacted, his name leaped from the page. I picked up the telephone and called him, mentioned our mutual friend, and scheduled lunch.

A few days later, I sat in a Vietnamese restaurant listening to him describe the rather amazing series of events that had led to the position he currently held. After hot food and cool stories, he gave me the names of several trusted recruiters, all of them unfamiliar to me. I went home and wrote to the recruiters. Within twenty-four hours of having received my letters, two out of three called. One was working on a job search in my field. He was near the end of the process, but liked what he saw on my résumé. He also liked what he heard as I described myself and my experience. I interviewed the next day and returned for more interviews two business days later.

As I stood at the elevator, preparing to leave following the second set of interviews, I asked the hiring manager about the time frame for making a decision. He looked at his watch and said, "We'll be making a decision in about…twenty minutes."

It was a thirty-five minute drive home. The phone rang as soon as I got there. They offered me the position. Not only was the offer a 20% increase in base pay over my previous position, but the position was both interesting and challenging.

I was stunned. I was also very much aware of the fact that if I had waited a day or two to make that first call, the one to the man I had delayed contacting for months, the rest of the story would have ended differently. The job would have been offered to someone else. The Universe had given me a nudge, I had made the call, and the rest was pure synchronicity.

Putting It Together

As discussed earlier, people tend to be helpful. There is something fundamental in the average person that enjoys being asked to help, particularly when that help can be provided quickly and easily. Most people love to think they have something desirable to share with others. Your chances are also very, very good that any person you contact for networking purposes has re-examined their own career and/or has been in job search within the past few years and remembers what it is like.

But *nothing* happens until you make contact. While most of us have become comfortable, and even dependent, on e-mail for making contact, save the e-mail contact for those already in your network with whom you have kept in touch. If you have become seriously out of touch with someone in your network (translate that to mean more than a year since you made contact), pick up the telephone and give them a call. A live connection is more personal and will acknowledge that you do honor the relationship, even though it has been some time since you have made contact.

Likewise, if you are calling someone whose name and contact information you have discovered on the Internet or some other research vehicle, contact him by telephone if you have that information. An e-mail to someone you do not know may be overlooked, ignored, or erased by its receiver.

What about those whose names and contact information have been given you by people in your network? Pick up the telephone and give them a call. These days, you are likely to get a voice messaging system, but you just might get them live, particularly if you call on the fringes of normal business hours. Keep it short and to the point. Let them know who suggested you give them a call, let them know the purpose of your call, and ask if you can schedule some time to either have a telephone conversation or meet with them. They *may* want to have the conversation over the phone instead of in person, but your chances of making a strong connection will be better if you can meet with them face to face. Offer to buy them lunch or a cup of coffee. Particularly with recruiters, it is important to present yourself face to face, if possible.

But be sensitive to the time demands facing *all* your networking contacts. Do not promise that you will take only ten minutes of their time in a face-to-face meeting. They will know better. *No* face-to-face meeting of any substance can be accomplished in less than thirty minutes and career networking meetings most frequently take longer than that.

If meeting face to face is not possible or practical, take advantage of any opportunity to talk over the telephone, whether it is a five-minute conversation on first contact or a scheduled callback time. If your initial call manages to reach the person live, checking to see if it is a good time to talk demonstrates your sensitivity to her time. She will appreciate it and you will improve your chances of receiving an equal measure of sensitivity in return.

One of the things I do not suggest is the overworked and timeworn ploy of requesting an *informational interview*. The very phrase may put off anyone savvy enough to be of genuine assistance to you because they have experienced this kind of networking before. There is a quality of dishonesty about it. The person making the request is often less interested in information about an industry, occupation or geographical location than they are interested in knowing whether or not *that* person or *that* company will give them a job. Even if they are true to the stated intent, few professionals have the time to spend with folks who are trolling for a new line of work, new industry to break into or new town to live in. Those trolling tend to be unfocused, have little invested in their own process, and are time wasters.

What if you really *are* contemplating a major career change and looking for information about career fields or industries? First, do your homework before you begin to make calls. Check into the field/industry on the Internet, read books about it, and learn the educational/training requirements for that line of work. Examine yourself and your proclivities. A person who hates being outdoors will probably be unhappy as a Park Ranger! Give some thought to what you want/need to know and put together some questions.

When you then call someone on your list of contacts, you will be better prepared and more likely to get a positive response from them. Let them know you are contemplating a change of career and/or industry focus and have done some research. Explain that their name was given to you as someone who is actually *in* that field/industry and that you would love to talk with them both to get a flavor for what it is like on the inside and to field the many questions you have as a result of your homework. It will be clear that you are doing more than trolling.

What do you do instead of using a gimmick like a request for an informational interview if what you are really wanting is to make solid connections that could further your career? The first thing you do is remind yourself of your own purpose. You are trying to get those molecules moving, bumping into one another. You are looking for leads. You are trying to determine if the person you are contacting has information or ideas for you or can direct you to someone who does. You are also a member of the human race reaching out to touch another member of the human race, genuinely, with good will, good humor, and the light of your own being shining through.

This last purpose is the one to keep foremost in your thinking. Your job is to do the work, make the calls, and enjoy the process. Your job is to enjoy and be thankful for the journey itself, so much so that the destination, while always somewhere in your mind, becomes a happy and eventual denouement in the story of your journey but not the reason for putting one foot in front of the other each day. You relish the journey itself and the people you meet on it.

When you remind yourself of this last and most important purpose, you will find that you are able to surrender to the process, detach from any particular outcome, and be your genuine self with whomever you meet on the journey. As a bonus, you just might make some friends along the way.

Networking is both a left brained and a right brained activity. The rational, logical, sequential part of you makes lists, schedules time to make contacts and follows through. The intuitive, holistic part of you treats the entire process as a grand flow of activity, as swirling energy within the larger Universe. That part stays softly alert, is gently aware of unusual and unexpected connections, expects synchronicity, and captures the moment.

Stay engaged and gently focused in any networking conversation. Trust and accept that you have something to offer in any interaction. Trust also that your networking contact will also have something to offer. It may be an idea, a suggestion, a job or the names of two or three other people you should contact. Stay on purpose but also allow yourself to be interested enough in the other and what they have to share with you that you stay in the flow of conversation, detached from your personal worries and needs, detached from any particular outcome. Once you are able to do this, you will relax enough to be your genuine self, and nothing is more compelling or interesting than the genuine article, however it is packaged.

After any networking contact, whether by telephone or face to face, *do* send a thank-you note to the person who graciously gave you her time and ideas. Yes, you can send it by e-mail, but good quality stationery and a hand-written note still make a favorable impression. Beyond the thank-you, *stay in touch with the person*. A network is not made by one contact, but by ongoing contact and relationships that are nurtured. Nurturing relationships means, among other things, that *you* are available when the *other* wants a networking meeting with you, too. Today you may be on the receiving end of assistance and tomorrow you may be on its giving end. This is not only how it works with relationships, but it is how the entire hoop of life works!

Chapter 8

MARKETING YOURSELF

...you live in a fundamentally friendly Universe that wants to receive your gifts of skills, talents, and hard work.

You ou have a passport, you have a visa, you have assessed where you want your travels to take you, and you have begun to meet new and interesting people on your journey. Now you want to explore the possibilities. What do you do? If you have done the work to this point, it is time to market yourself. This is one place where the only thing that can stand in your way is...you. Your willingness to do the work will be what makes the difference.

> A small group of people is gathered in a semicircle around a famous Toltec shaman and author. Some of these people will be spending the weekend in workshop with her. Others are there because they want to know more about shamanism or just want to see someone who spent time with Don Juan, the Toltec shaman made famous by Carlos Castaneda.
>
> After the speaker talks about her personal experience and offers some thoughts about shamanism, she opens it up for questions. Someone asks her what she views as the major impediments to setting intent. Without a pause, and with a tone of assurance, the first thing she says is, "Guts!"

Where marketing yourself is concerned, one of the greatest impediments is a lack of courage. Even people who are comfortable marketing the goods and services of businesses often have a difficult time marketing themselves. It is personal. To market yourself requires your deep understanding and appreciation of what you have to offer a potential employer. It requires the ability to discern which companies might need what you have to offer and the willingness to articulate why and how you may be just what they need. Assuming you have done your homework, have cleared internal impediments, and have a résumé that is a sparkling representation of what you have accomplished professionally, it still takes *guts* to market yourself in a world that is often more willing to close doors on you than willing to open them up and invite you in.

Organizations *need* good people to get business done. An incredible amount of thought, effort and money goes into staffing most organizations. There is a need for what you have to offer. Marketing yourself dovetails that need with your abilities. The problem, the need for courage, arises when you forget you live in a fundamentally friendly Universe that wants to receive your gifts of skills, talents, and hard work. With that forgetting, the marketing effort becomes an almost combative endeavor in which you bolster yourself to fight your way into the next job. In reality, because you *do* live in a friendly Universe, it is actually a delicious treasure hunt.

If you have not done the self-exploration, homework, clearing, or process of aligning yourself energetically, then stop and return to that work. Without that preparation, you are at the mercy of whatever drifts in front of your field of view. You will be less prepared to *brand* yourself. You may select opportunities that are inappropriate for you or, worse, you may simply allow all the selection to be done by the potential employer instead of remembering that it is as much your job to select the employer as it is the employer's job to select you.

If you *have* done the work to this point, then take a deep breath, remember that the Universe is a friendly place, remember that you have a gift to offer the world of work, and move forward from that place of remembering.

Take the marketing process seriously, but do not take it so seriously that you begin to take *yourself* too seriously. We are all bigger than we know and, at the same time, we are all simple pilgrims going down the road. The paradox of this is worth remembering and you will have an easier time remembering it if you market your *self* and not a slick marketing version of yourself.

Taking the marketing process seriously means, among other things, that you apply focus and organization to your efforts. While you *could* use a shotgun approach to marketing yourself, spreading *paper*—your résumé—everywhere, that is probably not the most focused way to approach the marketing effort. Target organizations. What have you learned about yourself from the self-exploration homework you have done? *What kinds* of organizations are appropriate for you? *Where* are those organizations? *Who* are they? *What* are their current needs and what are the current market conditions affecting your self-marketing effort?

Discerning who to market yourself to is easier today than ever before, thanks to both the Internet and the wide variety of business tabloids and journals at every newsstand. With a bit of effort, you can become relatively sophisticated about your personal market, whether it is local, regional or national. You will not become sophisticated, however, by sitting back and watching daytime television, waiting for the perfect opportunity to find *you*.

Yes, it *is* important to tap into the power of the Universe, align yourself with Universal Principles, become sensitive to synchronicity, and invite your future to approach you. But one unavoidable Universal Principle is the Law of Action.

We all have a wealth of Universal Guidance available to us. Depending upon your religious proclivities, you may think of that Guidance as God, the Virgin Mary, Mohammed, Buddha, your Spirit Guides, your Guardian Angel, your Higher Self, or some other articulation of enlightened mastership and the power of the Oneness. The Law of Action is as follows: The loving Guidance and assistance available to you is generally not available until you do something, *anything*, to help yourself.

Once you take a genuine step on your own behalf, the heavens open up and all Guidance available to you is empowered to act on your behalf. Why does it work this way? I do not have an answer to that; I only know that is *does* work this way. You need not like it, but you do need to accept it graciously.

Further, there is a relationship between the amount and quality of Guidance available and the amount and quality of effort on our own behalf. Ongoing action on your own behalf is necessary if you want to optimize the Guidance and help available to you. Help yourself and help your guidance help you. Do the work to determine your target market and begin to market yourself to it.

When it comes to sourcing potential jobs, the best source is the one that lands you the perfect job. Unfortunately, you will not know what that is until you *have* that perfect job. So what do you do? Do everything! Within the definition of *everything* are the following sources for the perfect job:

- The Internet
- Networking Leads
- Newspaper Ads
- Targeted Letter/Call Campaigns
- Search Firms
- Placement Offices
- Professional Organization Leads
- Chambers of Commerce
- Articles from Business/Professional Journals
- Career Fairs
- Internships
- Temporary Agencies
- Community Groups
- Volunteer Activities
- Alumni Organizations

- Trade Shows
- Conferences/Seminars

This list is by no means exhaustive; it provides merely a taste of the variety of ways in which people have sourced great jobs. It has probably occurred to you that, having dedicated an entire chapter to networking, I put a great deal of stock in it. That is true. In my experience, the single most important thing you can do to source the perfect job and market your way into it is to network. But while it may be the single most important thing you can do, it is far less effective by itself than it is when you practice networking as one among many methods of marketing yourself.

To maximize the potential of your self-marketing effort, begin to view the entire sphere of daily activity as a potential source for the next great position. Just as every interaction is an opportunity for networking, when you begin to think of it in those terms, every interaction with the world around you can be part of the fact-finding related to sourcing the next job.

Even the simplest of things you do in the process of marketing yourself adds to the energy of attracting the perfect job. One simple thing adds energy to the process. The second thing brings additional energy to interact with the first. The third thing brings even more energy, and so on.

Allow that knowing to inspire you and bring a playful quality to the process. This *is* a treasure hunt, after all. Do your research. Become familiar with the companies in the market you wish to enter. Discover what is, or could be, available for you in them. Remember that what is not currently available can become available tomorrow or next week. Stay alert.

Look for the hidden opportunities, those not widely advertised or even thought of by most people in search. If some aspect of your life is particularly important to you, get on the Internet and explore the sites relating to it. Are you devoutly Christian and desire a position with an organization in which this will be seen as an asset and not a liability? Do you know that there are many Internet sites devoted to job search for Christians? Are you interested in working for a small company with a newly developing need for what you have to offer? Did you know that the Executive Directors for many Chambers of Commerce have an insider's grasp on which companies within their Chamber are growing, changing, and otherwise stretching in ways that may fit with what you have to offer? Are you a CFO looking for the next creative engagement? If so, are you a member of the Financial Executives Institute and did you know that your local chapter may have a sub-group focused on helping CFOs in job search?

Sometimes the best marketing efforts happen while you are otherwise engaged in living your life.

In an act of innocence and courage, Melissa moved from Buffalo, New York to Colorado. She knew virtually no one in Colorado and had no job prospects, but had decided to live in a part of the country that appealed to her and her active lifestyle. A conversation with a recruiter led to a meeting with a career coach and she was on her way.

During their work together, the coach suggested that Melissa spend some time during her search doing volunteer work. Not only would it be an excellent way to meet people and help her hone her networking skills, it would also be an act of service, a way to contribute to the community.

Melissa took this suggestion seriously and a bit of magic happened. A lover of cats, Melissa shared her life with two. A rescue shelter for unwanted animals, the Max Fund, appealed to her as a group with whom she might enjoy volunteering some time. Melissa's vocational aspirations had nothing to do with animals in need of rescue. A lawyer with an MBA and a small amount of experience in marketing while in graduate school, Melissa was looking for an opportunity to break into the marketing arena in Denver.

While cleaning up after a successful fundraiser for the Max Fund, Melissa found herself in conversation with some other volunteers. She talked about her recent move to Denver and her search for a marketing job. One of the other volunteers just happened to be the president-elect of the local chapter of the American Marketing Association (AMA). She and Melissa scheduled a date for coffee.

Melissa's new acquaintance and fellow volunteer came to that coffee date with the names of four people she thought Melissa should call for networking purposes. One of them was the current president of the Denver AMA.

Melissa, dazed by her good fortune in meeting people directly connected with the marketing field, called the chapter president and arranged to meet with him. When they met, Melissa spent an hour describing her background and what she was looking for in a job. A rapport developed quickly between the two and the conversation seemed effortless, like talk between friends. Finally he asked, "So, what is it that you want from *me*?"

Without hesitation, Melissa replied, "A job!"

"Okay," he responded.

As the fates would have it, John, the president of the local chapter of AMA, had recently taken a position as Director of Sales and Marketing for a small company. He needed staff and was in a position to hire. Melissa had just successfully marketed *herself* into her first marketing position in Denver.

Melissa's first marketing position in Denver did not just drop into her lap. She worked hard before the magic began to happen and her concentrated efforts helped make the magic possible. When she began to market herself, she scouted the Internet, newspapers, business journals and other sources of information. She networked and she talked with recruiters. She targeted companies by size, location, industry, and culture. She targeted specific jobs. Melissa prepared and practiced a three-minute summary of her life and experience. She examined anything in her voice and body language that could work against her. She looked at what fed her self-confidence and what detracted from it, doing more of the former and less of the latter.

Admittedly, Melissa had moments, hours, and days of feeling discouraged, but even when she was discouraged she exhibited courage by doing a number of things: she kept putting one foot in front of the other, kept up the marketing effort; she took care of herself, attending to her physical and emotional needs; she maintained a healthy sense of humor; she became familiar with the community; she balanced the work of looking for a job with a healthy dose of relaxation and play, and; she took seriously the fact that every encounter, every activity, is part of the treasure hunt that results in the perfect job.

Boldly asking for a job of everyone with whom you network is *not* something I endorse. If you are overly focused on the destination—the job—you cannot maintain the necessary detachment that allows you to be genuine. But in Melissa's case, the alchemy she created through hard work and integrity of spirit crafted a bit of magic that ultimately led to that fateful question and answer.

Marketing yourself *is* both an alchemical process and a treasure hunt. Courage, integrity, and hard work will transform your beautiful essence into a beautiful essence with a new opportunity for creative engagement with whatever organization that constitutes what is true treasure for *you*.

Chapter 9

THE INTERVIEW

What you intend for yourself is that your highest good,
and the highest good of others, be served in the process
of the meeting. The outcome will take care of itself.

Journeys provide many opportunities to meet people. Sometimes they speak English and sometimes they speak another language entirely. Good intentions and good will go a long way when meeting people, whether or not you speak the same language. Your energy field has the remarkable ability to send out the essence of who you are. When your career exploration journey leads you to the inevitable place of being asked to meet face to face with someone for purposes of determining whether you and the organization s/he represents are a fit, you can get tied up in knots, worrying about selling yourself, or you can view it as a chance to meet another pilgrim on the journey. The choice is yours.

There *are*, of course, some advantages to having a date/time set for a meeting. When that meeting is an interview, it gives you an opportunity to prepare by:

- Setting your intent and becoming both centered and grounded;
- Anticipating and planning for the discussion;
- Dressing appropriately, and;
- Eating something that will sustain you beforehand and otherwise tending to the needs of your body.

Setting Your Intent

Many people approach the interview as would an actor going to an audition. They view it as an opportunity to trot out their talents and gifts and to demonstrate how and why they are the perfect person for the organization. This is not an entirely wrong approach, but it misses a crucial point and is not the optimal way to set your intent.

What you are seeking is the perfect position for you in the optimal organization, at least for this moment in time. You do not need to force-fit something that is perfect for you. It will fall into place quite naturally, as if some force of nature draws you and the organization together. In other words, hard-selling yourself is worse than unnecessary; it is counterproductive.

There is good news in this. Relax. Return to the chapter on networking and remind yourself that the best possible outcome will be provided by remembering that you are meeting with other human beings, fellow pilgrims on the road of life. Remind yourself that you have something to offer in any interaction. Remind yourself that if you become so interested in the person or persons you are meeting and in the organization itself, all self-consciousness will fall away and you will present your genuine self. What you intend for yourself is that your highest good, and the highest good of others, be served in the process of this meeting. The outcome will take care of itself.

Take a deep breath. Become centered and grounded within yourself.

Centering And Grounding

1. Stand in a relaxed posture, spine straight but not rigid, knees slightly flexed. Close your eyes.
2. Take a few deep breaths, breathing in through the nose, allowing your belly to expand with the in-breath, breathing out through your

mouth, allowing your belly to contract with the out-breath.

3. Focus your attention on that place in your body that is approximately two inches below your navel and just a bit in front of your spine. Feel the stability provided you when your attention is placed in this area. Feel the power of it.

4. Now, maintaining this sense of centeredness, imagine the top of your head, your crown chakra, opening like a blossom, allowing Divine light to enter you.

5. Imagine this light filtering through your entire body, permeating each cell and each molecule, flowing downward from the top of your head to your face, throat, chest cavity, arms, abdomen, and legs, filling you with light.

6. Now envision that same light passing through your body and into the solid ground on which you stand. Your body is permeated with the light, which continues to flow into the top of your head. Every part of your being absorbs the light. There is so much light that it passes freely through you and enters Mother Earth.

7. Feel the connection between the Divine Source of the light, your body, and Mother Earth. Above, below and within are joined in the blissful, life-giving light. You feel the power of your energetic center (that point below your navel), you feel your connection to the life-giving energy flowing into you from above, and you experience a comforting feeling of solidity and groundedness in your connection with Mother Earth.

This centering and grounding exercise is useful preparation for almost anything: the beginning of the new day, meetings with people, difficult tasks ahead, or anything else that would be helped by fully occupying your physical body and experiencing its place in the Universe.

Set the intent that you will be guided by your own internal gyroscope to the perfect experience and outcome, that which satisfies your highest good and the highest good for those with whom you will interact, whatever those are. Then detach yourself from all expectation, knowing that all will unfold perfectly.

Anticipating And Planning For The Discussion

Remembering a few truths about yourself and other humans, centering and grounding, and setting your intent comprise a healthy foundation for your preparations. Once you have done these things, though, you are not done. The thinking side of you will want preparation for the interview now that the foundation laid has satisfied your spirit and emotions.

If you have reached the interview stage, you have probably already done many things that will serve to prepare you. But if you have not yet researched the company, it is time to do so. Sometimes an opportunity for an interview comes as if by magic, with little contact or work on your part. It is a beautiful thing when it happens, and when it happens, you have probably not yet had a chance to thoroughly research the company before the offer for an interview is made. It would be a mistake, however, to fail to do so before the interview itself.

Check out the company by examining their web site, talking with anyone you know who knows something about the company, reviewing their annual report, talking with your investment broker about their track record, getting an opinion from the head of the local Chamber of Commerce—virtually any way you can. Doing so will accomplish a number of things:

- Research will give you information that will help you decide if this is the organization for you;
- Research will give you a sense of who the corporate players are as well as the products and/or services the organization has to offer;
- Research will provide you with information on which to base questions, should you have the opportunity to ask them, and;
- Research will demonstrate to the interviewer that you care enough about the company to learn something about it and are smart

enough to have done your homework; and you can bet these last two things will suggest to them the kind of employee you will likely be!

Next, review all the work you have done to understand yourself, your style, your talents, and your gifts. If you have done the exercises and homework suggested thus far, now is a good time to review that work. If you have taken a personality assessment tool (like The Birkman Method®), refresh your memory about your major learnings from it.

Third, prepare yourself for possible interview questions. There are dozens of books covering this subject and I am not going to provide you with a template. I will suggest, though, that you prepare for several types of questions:

- Open ended questions about you and your life such as, *Can you tell me something about yourself?* It is extremely important that you come to any interview with a three-minute summary of your life, your experience, and the top few achievements of which you are proudest. Practice this, standing in front of a mirror, if necessary. You do not want to sound rehearsed, but you do want to be able to answer this question effortlessly.

- Résumé based questions about what you have done and the outcomes of what you have done (your experience, in other words), your training, your level of expertise in given areas, lapses in time-frames on the résumé, and similar inquiries that flow rather naturally from the résumé and cover letter.

- Behavioral based questions relating to your style and the way in which you have handled relevant life/work situations in the past. As with general questions about your life, these questions tend to be open ended; that is, they cannot be answered with a *yes* or *no* response. If the interviewer is shrewd, these questions will be based on your actual experience and not how you might handle a hypothetical situation. In other words, the interviewer will ask you to *tell me about a time when...* The interviewer may be seeking information about how you communicate, your leadership style, how you handle conflict, or any other behavioral area that has relevance to the job.

Fourth, and most important, *do whatever is uplifting, relaxing, refreshing, renewing, and inspiring to you* as a part of your preparation. By taking care of yourself, you will present with more self-confidence, ease, and congruity.

Laura had an important interview scheduled for the next day. She was excited about it and a bit anxious. Laura placed a call to her career coach, Don, to advise him of the upcoming interview. Don was pleased for her and supportive, offering a few reminders on what she might do to prepare.

Laura hung up from her conversation with Don feeling only a slight lessening of the knots in her stomach. She tried to prepare for possible interview questions by pacing around her family room, thinking of likely questions and appropriate answers, but she was too restless to concentrate for long.

Finally, Laura gave up and decided to prepare for the interview while taking a hike. She might as well be out in nature while she prepared, she thought. Laura drove to her favorite hiking trail and hiked for several hours. The air held the crispness of autumn and leaves crunched beneath her feet. She saw deer feeding in a grove of trees on a nearby hill. It felt good to use her body.

Laura did use the time hiking to think through potential interview questions and how she might answer them. She also reminded herself of her inherent goodness and her desire to find what would be *right work* for her. Mostly, though, she breathed deeply, worked up a sweat on the challenging uphill grade, enjoyed the beauty of nature, and found herself grateful for the opportunity her job search had provided her to hike during the middle of an erstwhile work day.

Laura felt refreshed and renewed from the hike. The interview the following day went extremely well. Laura called Don after the interview and her relaxed, enthused state of being was obvious in her voice. Don was impressed by how well Laura had handled herself. Laura was impressed, too.

Laura did admit, rather sheepishly, that she had *wasted* some time the day before by taking a hike. She attempted to defend herself by telling Don that she had actually done some of the preparation work while on the hike, but admitted spending most of the time enjoying the pure pleasure of the hike itself.

The response Laura got from Don was not what she expected.

"Laura," Don said, "I want you to listen to me quite carefully. I talked with you yesterday before that hike and I'm talking with you today, after the hike and after the interview. Something important has shifted in you during that time. My guess is that the change in you, which I can even hear in your voice, is not a result of the interview so much as the hike. In fact, I would bet that the interview went as well as it did *because* you took that hike. So, from now on, I don't want you to think of hikes before interviews as time wasters. For you, they are a valid part of the preparation!"

Dressing Appropriately

Even for those with a good sense of style and a history of dressing appropriately for all occasions, choosing the appropriate attire for an interview can be a challenge. Organizations have cultures that seem to be translated into a kind of culturally accepted style. Unless you have had the opportunity to see or hear about the organization's attire-style before the interview, you may have to do some guesswork. Some interviewers will give candidates a heads-up as to what is acceptable and appropriate attire for the interview, and it is a kindness when they do so. More often than not, though, you are on your own.

How do you determine what is appropriate? First, take your cues from what you know about the organization. Even with today's relaxed rules around attire, some industries and kinds of organizations are more conservative and formal in attire than others. Would you dress for an interview at an old, revered banking establishment in the same attire as you would for an interview at a high-tech, start-up company? Maybe, but probably not.

Next, dress in clothing that suits you and represents your personal sense of style, without being too *outré* or trendy, unless you are interviewing for the rare position that assumes the candidates will be so attired. This is not the time to make a political or social statement through your appearance, but it is also not the time to dress in a style that is foreign to you, simply because you think it will fit in. The first approach will get you noticed, but probably not favorably; the second approach fails to honor your uniqueness and will probably be noticed because something about you does not seem to be congruent.

Choose attire that fits your style and does so in a way that does not distract from the business at hand. I once stopped dead in my tracks upon seeing a candidate sitting in the lobby of a company at which I worked, waiting for his interview with one of the company executives. He wore a rather baggy, ill-fitting suit…and a pair of sneakers. It was amusing, I must admit. He did not look comfortable and he did not look used to this attire. I could not imagine what he had been thinking as he dressed for the interview.

As for color and pattern, I have heard many theories about which colors will be most effective in an interview. I am not sure that any of them are more important than wearing something appropriate that you feel good about and good in. Can black be viewed as intimidating? That has been suggested. Is navy blue the quintessential interview color? Maybe, but what if you neither like navy blue nor feel good in it? Does the pinstriped suit represent power? Maybe, but in some quarters it is thought to be a pattern that elicits stress in the person looking at it, while plaids are thought to provide a sense of relief because they elicit a whole-brain response. Allow good taste and appropriateness to dictate color and pattern. If you have doubts about what to wear, pick something you think might be right and ask for an assessment by someone you know who always looks appropriate.

What about personal grooming? Do we even need to address this? Yes, be clean and neat. Do not overdo *anything*: aftershave (in fact, it is a good idea to forego aftershave or perfume, as some people are allergic to them), hairstyle, makeup, or jewelry/watch. You want your uniqueness to shine, and that means keeping the focus more on you than on your accoutrements.

Fueling Yourself For The Interview

I am not a doctor and I do not have a degree in nutrition. This is not medical advice. It never ceases to amaze me, though, how frequently people prepare in every other way for an interview and yet ignore the issue of fueling their body as part of the preparation. Athletes attend to what they eat as part of their preparation for important athletic events. Should you be any different in your preparation for the interview?

Eat something that will sustain you prior to the interview, without eating so much that you are uncomfortable. Protein is good because it has staying power.

Fuel your body by building your energy through proper sleep before the interview. If you are over-tired, you are not going to look your best and your brain will not be as sharp.

Finally, do anything else that constitutes taking care of your body. The preparation period before the interview is a time to enlist the aid of your physical self by caring for it.

The Interview Itself

You have done your preparatory work and you have arrived for your interview, just a little ahead of the appointed time so you can use the restroom, collect your thoughts, complete an application for employment if required, and relax. Now...relax.

Step into your full self. Your career and your life are not dependent on this one interview, though it may feel that way if you have been in search for the perfect opportunity a long time. It is extremely important to detach yourself from expectations of any particular outcome. Remember that you and the perfect job will find one another. This may be it, or it may not. Either way, use the experience as an opportunity to have a joyful interaction with another human being. Use the experience to hone your interview skills and practice the fine art of intuition. Remind yourself that you have already done a number of things that made you an appealing candidate for the organization or you would not have been invited to the interview in the first place.

When the interviewer greets you, have a smile on your face and extend your hand for a handshake. Handshakes are important and sometimes done poorly by otherwise competent people. Do not just touch fingertips or extend only half of the hand. You do not want to half-heartedly greet the interviewer, so do not offer a half-hearted handshake. Offer your whole hand. Do not grip the interviewer's hand as if in the first stages of an arm-wrestling competition and do not offer a limp hand. Use a firm but not hand-breaking grip. Human touch should be pleasant and your handshake should speak well of you.

Follow the interviewer's lead graciously. Sit where motioned to sit. Accept a glass of water if offered. A well lubricated throat will make speaking easier. It is common for interviewers to engage in small talk for a brief time as a method for helping the interviewee feel at ease. Be willing to talk about the weather or last night's football game, but keep your responses brief. You want to be engaged with the interviewer, but you do not want to appear unfocused about the purpose of the visit, which is to discuss the job and your candidacy for it.

Then allow yourself to shine as the interview commences. You will shine if you allow yourself to forget about *proving* anything and just give your genuine self room to express itself. You will shine if you are genuinely interested in what the interviewer says about the organization and asks about you…and show it. You will do that if you trust your preparation and trust that this job is yours if it is meant to be.

Be truthful in your answers to questions. That does not mean you must offer details that reflect badly on you and it does not mean that you should treat the interviewer as you would your therapist. Be tactful, be complete, and be brief enough in your replies that you retain the attention of the interviewer.

Some books and coaches will advise you to keep the interviewer talking more than 50% of the time. I find this to be bad advice. Good interviewers will attempt to keep you talking at least 75% of the interview time. There is much to be covered if the interviewer is going to have the data needed to make a good assessment and the well prepared interviewer will want to stay on purpose.

But what if the interviewer does not appear to be skilled in the art and science of interviewing? Then, my friend, *you* will need to keep the interview on purpose. Ask if explanations or examples would be helpful. Find ways to fold the important behavioral qualities and significant outcomes/experiences into the dialogue. Be compassionate. Interviews can be stressful for the interviewer as well as the interviewee.

Allow yourself enough time to formulate an answer to a question in your mind before opening your mouth. Speaking without thinking is a dangerous practice in an interview. Few interviewers will expect you to answer an interview question without pausing to consider the answer. That does not mean you should look blankly or sheepishly at the interviewer, squirming in your seat for two minutes, if you do not have an answer. If you are asked for an example and cannot think of one after pausing to contemplate, tell the interviewer that a good example is not coming to mind. Again, be honest. *Do not* make something up. The interviewer may encourage you to give it a bit more thought or may go on to the next question.

You may have time to ask questions of your own. If given the opportunity, have some questions ready. No, do not ask about pay or benefits. You will appear to be more interested in the prospects for personal gain than the job itself. Do ask questions about the company based on the research you did in preparation for the interview.

When the interview is over, express your appreciation for the interviewer's time. Unless this is one of those rare occasions when you are clear that this is not the job for you, let the interviewer know you are excited about the opportunity. If you are feeling a bit uncertain about the job, still express enthusiasm. You want to leave your options open. More than once, I have seen someone initially squeamish only to find, by the end of the selection process, that they are quite excited about the job. If this *is* one of those rare occasions when you have somehow made it to the interview phase of selection and discover, through the interview process, that this is not the job for you, thank the interviewer for his/her time and for helping you assess that this is probably not the opportunity you are seeking. Wish the company the best. Whether or not you end up working for this company, you want them to remember you with a sense of respect.

Have respect for the interviewer's time when the interview is over. Make a graceful exit. Offer your hand for a handshake as you did when you met. If the interviewer has not given you a sense of timing and process steps towards completion of the selection process, ask what you can expect to happen next. This will also demonstrate an interest in the job and your candidacy for it.

After The Interview

First, congratulate yourself. You were offered the opportunity for an interview, a success in and of itself. You prepared for it, you relaxed, and you did just fine. Celebrate that.

As soon as is practical after the interview, take notes. Go to a coffee shop, sit in your car, or do it as soon as you get home. Record interesting and/or new questions asked of you during the interview, answers to questions that might come up again, information about the company, reflections about the interviewer, and anything else you will want to remember later. It is amazing how quickly the details of an interview are lost if you do not record them! The interviewer probably took notes during the interview. And even if you jotted a few notes yourself, now is the time to capture everything that may be helpful later.

Write a thank you note within twenty-four to forty-eight hours of the interview. Yes, you may do it via e-mail, although hard copy is always a nice touch. Thank the interviewer for his/her time and express your continued interest in the position. Do not stop there. Include something specific and personal: a reflection about the company, something that struck you about the interviewer and/or a statement made by him/her, *anything* that shows you were engaged, interested, and reflective during and after the interview. It is also useful to couple your interest in the company with your best wishes for their success, regardless of the outcome of this selection process. Writing a thank you letter will differentiate you from the legions who fail to do so. Expressing your best wishes, whether or not the organization extends you a job offer, makes you a classy human being. Keep the entire tone genuine; speak from the heart as well as the head. This is not a form letter, but a letter of gratitude from one human being to another.

I once told my interviewer, in the thank you note, that I thought he had a quiet strength that would continue to serve the company well. I meant it. It was from the heart. I got the job. Later, someone at the company told me that when he received my thank you note, he came into her office, grinning widely, and read it to her. It meant something to him. It just so happens that the interviewer was also my first boss at that company!

Above all else, allow yourself to become a bit detached after the interview. You have done your best. If the job is meant for you, it will come to you. If not, something better awaits you, something perfect for you. Obsessing about the opportunity will not bring it closer. In fact, obsessing will create a roadblock. Surrender to the delicious possibilities that await you, whether in this job or another.

As I said at the beginning of this chapter, the interview is an opportunity to meet another pilgrim on road of life. When you prepare, relax, detach from outcome, and remember that the journey is as important as the outcome, interviews can become remarkable opportunities to meet fellow pilgrims. Sometimes you are even offered a job!

Chapter 10

MOTHER TOLD ME
THERE WOULD BE DAYS LIKE THIS

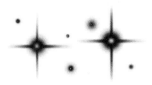

Transformation is uncomfortable,
disconcerting, unsettling, and necessary in life.

No matter how well you plan a journey, life happens. Schedules change, the weather is unpredictable, options change, some opportunities disappear as if they had never existed at all, and people with whom you thought you might connect are out of the country when you arrive. Plans you thought were confirmed seem to have been made through the Buddhist sand mandala process, gone with a movement of the hand as soon as completed. The bottom drops out of the dollar and the currency you brought with you does not seem to be worth as much as you thought it would be. You thought you had a passing ability to speak the local language, but you find yourself befuddled by the local dialect.

The career exploration/job search journey is like that, too. Some days you find yourself muttering to your cat, your best friend, or to yourself in a mirror "Mother *told* me there would be days like this." Maybe the selection process in which you have been a prime candidate is brought to a screeching halt due to a downturn in the economy or because someone else has been selected for the position. Perhaps you have just heard about the perfect job *after* it has been filled. You might be beginning to doubt your value in the current market. Maybe you feel as if your best networking and communication skills have done nothing to calm fears that you are invisible and inaudible, as if a disembodied spirit instead of a living human being.

Whatever the reason, every career journey has days like this. Your spouse or best friend may tell you to get over yourself or they may tell you to intensify your efforts. Either way, you are likely to feel frustrated and that frustration will be heightened if the current experience and your feelings about it continue for a week, a month, or more.

So what do you do? Think of the many suggestions that follow as soul food à la carte. Scan the suggestions for those that seem tasty and sample them.

Realize That Divine Timing May Be At Work

Remember that Divine timing is not *your* timing. We humans tend to want things when we want them, which is usually sooner than later, and which is usually on our own terms. One of the problems with this proclivity is that it ignores the Divine alchemy at work in our lives. Magic frequently happens with a suddenness that makes one as dizzy as a childhood roll down a hill. That suddenness belies the lengthy process that usually precedes it. Miracles may happen in the blink of an eye, but they seldom happen overnight.

The work you have done to clear and understand yourself, to search out what is right work for you, to explore the market, and to forge new relationships in your network takes time to percolate energetically. Take a deep breath and allow that to happen. Many good things in life follow a meaningful pause; we just do not always realize how meaningful the pause has been until later.

Delays can be purposeful when the Universe conspires to meet your highest good. Try visualizing it in the following way. You have the courage to open a door to your innermost being. You push out of that door everything within that no longer fits for you, like a homeowner setting discarded household items on the front stoop for a charity to collect. You now have space to add the new and you welcome it. You leave that internal door open and wait. Nothing happens. Maybe you do the equivalent of taking a peek outside the front door of your home, looking up and down the street to see if what you are waiting for has just turned a corner and is about to pull into your driveway. Nothing is there. You continue to wait.

You do a bit more internal clearing and rearranging. Finally, you consider closing the door. You have waited a long time, after all. You think better of it and leave the door open. You want it to be easy for the new to find you when it comes. You go about the process of living and even forget, for a time, that the door is open and you have welcomed the new to enter. Every time you pass by that door, however, you notice it is open and you remember that what you are waiting for has not yet arrived.

You become impatient. You begin to wonder if you should have cleared away as much as you have and consider bringing some of what you set outside back in. You might even do that. It takes little time for you to realize, though, that what you had chosen to discard really did no longer suit you, so you clear it away again. And you wait.

Finally, when you are engaged in doing something with passion and verve, something that has nothing to do with what you have been waiting for (like tap dancing in the living room), there is a knock on the door. You go to the door and are amazed by what you find. You have been waiting for something of modest size, attractively packaged. The man who has you sign for what has arrived points to a semi parked in front of your house. He explains that what you have waited for took so long to get to you because: (1) it was custom-made, just for you; (2) it was crafted by experts with the best of materials and extreme care; and (3) it was bigger than anticipated, requiring a larger conveyance. Divine timing can work in just this way.

Take A Time Out

When the going gets tough, the tough go meditating…or hiking, or on a field trip to a museum, or anywhere else that feeds the soul. Sometimes the best thing to do is *nothing* related to the career. When you overly focus on your intent for an extended period, whether it is finding the perfect job or finding the perfect mate, the very energy of that focus can impede the process. At such times, the most useful thing to do is to switch the focus to anything that nourishes your being.

This is not a suggestion to drop out and give up the process, but a suggestion to take a brief time-out. A few hours or a day may do it. If you feel seriously stuck, consider a short road trip to somewhere you love or somewhere you have a desire to see for the first time. Just breaking your routine can powerfully shift the energy.

There is a time for doing and there is a time for being. But being and doing are not counterpoised and they are not counterpoints to one another. Each flows to and from the other. Optimally, what you do quite naturally flows from who you are. If the *doing* part of the flow is blocked, it may be useful to discern what may be blocking the flow between the *being* and the *doing*. You might find it useful to spend a part of your time-out exploring the possibility of such a block.

Have you lost your internal gyroscope and begun comparing yourself with others? You are *you*, not someone else. The expression of who you are in the world of doing is unique. Comparisons inevitably lead to judgments that assess relative value and there is no way to compare your value with anything outside yourself. The issue is how you are stacking up with yourself, not how you are stacking up in comparison to someone else's life.

Are you experiencing inertia? Sometimes the mere weight of habit, personal history, and comfort can keep you in a groove that may have fit some past version of you, but not the current one. There is good news here. Inertia, in Newtonian terms, ends when acted upon by an outside force. Inertia, in the physics of the human spirit, frequently ends when acted upon by an *inside* force. That force is an internal shift to correct the discomfort and dissonance between being and doing selves that are out of sync. There is a bonus when the shift takes place, because in both Newtonian physics and the physics of the human spirit, there is inertia of motion and inertia of rest. In other words, once you get past the block and begin to move, some momentum of the spirit seems to take over.

Larry had been in a quandary for some time. Not only did his career lack passion, *most of his life* lacked passion. After leaving a thoroughly unsatisfying job, Larry hired a career coach. The work they did together re-set his expectations. He began to think it was not only okay for him to feel passionate about his work, but optimal. Still, Larry found it difficult to become excited about his job search. Something was missing.

Among the things Larry took seriously from the career coaching work was the encouragement to step back and turn his attention to something other than his job search; to allow his intuitive self to advise him in moments when he was not focused on his career. Some part of him realized he had been suppressing passion for a long time and he wanted to regain that passion.

One of the extra-curricular things Larry wanted to conquer was Quandary Peak, one of Colorado's famous fourteeners—mountains over fourteen thousand feet high. He had first attempted the mountain some years earlier, a failed attempt that had inspired him to get back in shape. Then, earlier that year, he had made the attempt again. He had begun the ascent too late in the day and had been thwarted by an afternoon thunderstorm. Larry was determined to conquer Quandary Peak.

The morning of September 11, 2001, Larry learned of the terrorist attacks on the United States. He might have stayed glued to his television set, but he had already made plans to attempt another ascent of Quandary Peak and felt a strong urge to allow *nothing* to postpone this personal challenge. If ever there was a time to conquer the mountain—and his personal quandary—it was now.

Larry began his ascent at 10 AM, later than he would have liked but the best he could do under the circumstances. Somehow, he felt that if he could make it to the summit, he would be able to resolve his personal quandary, reclaim control of his life, and find the strength to survive whatever the world presented him.

Larry conquered Quandary Peak that day and in doing so, conquered his own quandaries. By mid to late September, he began to pursue stock trading, something for which he had felt passion for some time, but had not seriously considered. On October 1, 2001, Larry filed for divorce. While his marriage of long standing had once brought much joy to his life, it was now over. He had been avoiding that fact. To reclaim passion in his life, he needed to infuse his entire life with passion and he was committed to doing just that.

Larry's time-out had gained him the rest of his life!

Does Fear Have You In Its Grips?

Does fear have you in its grips? If so, of what are you afraid? If you are afraid of trying something and failing, you can stay safely ensconced wherever you currently are, and you will never know what you might have done. If you are less afraid of failing than succeeding, and afraid of both the responsibility and freedom that come with success, then stay stuck at your own risk. The Universe has a way of propelling us forward gently or with a sledgehammer, depending upon our willingness to move. Consider the possibility that the biggest risk may be not taking one.

There is a relationship between comfort level with taking risks and making mistakes. If you dare to dream and dream the dare into life: (1) you are probably going to have an interesting life; (2) you are probably going to make a fair number of mistakes; (3) you will likely learn a great deal; and (4) you may have the kind of *failures* that hone your skills and ultimately lead to success. If Thomas Edison had abandoned his work with the first failure, we might still be living in darkness!

I am not an advocate for wild abandonment in risk taking. One person's foolishness may be another person's daring, but there is a difference between ignorance and risk; a difference between unbridled immaturity and risk. You need to explore that difference for yourself. Try applying both your rational thinking skills and intuition to the situation, then give consideration to the possible consequences of failure. In other words, consider your options, ask for divine inspiration, and measure the distance to the bottom before jumping into the abyss; then go ahead and jump if you are willing to take the risk.

Seek Comfort From Family And Friends

Along with muttering, "Mother told me there would be days like this," you may be saying to yourself, "If ever I needed a friend, it is now." Life enfleshed in human form was not meant to be spent alone. Talk through your frustrations with an empathic soul, preferably someone who really cares about you, like a close friend or family member. Unless you have been relying on your friends and family members to keep your spirits aloft to an unreasonable extent, whoever you choose will likely be happy to lend an ear. In fact, they will probably feel a sense of relief at being able to do something to help you.

Relationships are maintained through acts of intimacy, interactions in which spirit speaks to spirit. If you simply want to express frustration or weariness with the process, let your listening partner know you are not looking for problem solving advice, only someone to listen while you express yourself. Humans are frequently ill trained to listen, but well trained to provide advice. You need to be clear on what you need. The act of listening at a deep level to a fellow traveler on life's journey is a gift to you from that person's spirit. Be willing to reciprocate at some future time.

Remember that you are human and allow yourself to have whatever feelings you are having without guilt or self-recrimination. Allow yourself to bask in the warmth of family and friends. You will likely find your feelings of frustration passing through you, replaced by an uplifting of spirit instead of becoming petrified and brittle inside.

Clear Your Physical Space

You have done internal clearing work, now look around you and see what can be cleared from your physical surroundings. Just as internal clearing makes the way for new energy in your life, external clearing seems to act out that process physically, magnifying the creation of energetic space for the new to enter.

Physical space has energy, just as people do. In the same way that humans may become physically, mentally, emotionally or spiritually stagnant, physical space can become energetically stagnant. Just as humans can hold pain within their bodies, they can energetically hold pain within the physical space in which they live. Humans can change the way they see themselves and the way they move through the world by changing hairstyles or attire. They can also change the way they see themselves and move through the world by changing the physical space they occupy every day.

Spend some time clearing the unneeded items and general clutter from a closet, your basement, the garage…or the entire house. Toss the junk and give the usable items to a charitable organization. If the house has become a bit dingy because your focus has been on your career more than your physical surroundings, spend some time cleaning until the house shines.

It is important for you to engage in the cleaning yourself and not just delegate the chore to a cleaning service, your children, or your spouse. Make a family project of it if you must, but put your own back into the work. You will deprive yourself of the power of this kind of clearing if you default to others. Do the cleaning mindfully, treating it as the sacred ceremony it is. Civilizations have relied on ceremony to create sacred space for millennia and cleaning the space is an important step in the process of creating sacred space.

Once you have finished cleaning, take time to *feel* the difference in the energy of the space. Notice any areas that feel energetically sluggish and use your intuition to advise you about what these areas may need. Open a few windows in the house to let in fresh air, even for a few minutes if it is very cold outside.

If you have incense or a sage bundle for smudging, walk through your newly clean house, carefully wafting smoke throughout. As you do, have the intent of purifying the space and sending prayers of gratitude for the sanctuary your home provides you. Spend some additional time in areas that continue to feel energetically sluggish.

If you do not have incense or a smudge stick, a bell, drum, or other musical instrument may be used in the same way. If you have nothing more than your own voice, use it as the powerful vehicle it is in sacred ceremony. Tone or chant. If none of these appeal to you, than create any ceremony that uses earth, air, fire, or water and appeals to sight, sound, smell, or touch to sanctify the space you have cleaned.

Once you feel a sense of purity and clearness to the space, bring in fresh flowers or an herb plant, add the sound of running water, or otherwise consciously keep the purified energy circulating.

You may be surprised at how profoundly the activities of cleaning and clearing physical space affect you. By giving the quality of freshness to the space around you, something profoundly fresh and decidedly salubrious can open within you, making the way for something good to become manifested in your life.

Caroline's job search was stalled. Leads evaporated. Interviews failed to produce job offers. No one seemed interested in her unique skill set. The holidays gave way to a new year and on January first, feeling mentally exhausted but physically restless, she looked around her apartment and began to notice the clutter she had been ignoring for months.

Caroline started with her bedroom closet and, three days later, had managed to clear the clutter from and clean every room in her apartment. In the process, she gathered a wide assortment of unused, unneeded, and unwanted articles. She donated these items to charity.

Feeling a sense of spaciousness, but still a sense of heaviness, she then rearranged her furniture and walked through the apartment with a smoldering bundle of sage, wafting its smoke into every corner and offering prayers of gratitude for her beautiful and newly clutter-free space.

Two days later, a recruiter contacted Caroline with the most interesting and potentially career enhancing job opportunity she had ever been presented.

Spend Time Learning

When you feel unable to generate what you want outside yourself, despite your best efforts, spend time generating new ideas and new skills by learning something. Upgrade your skills by learning a new piece of computer software or a foreign language. Take a college or adult education course. Ask a friend to teach you how to ski and teach your friend how to build a birdhouse. Not only will you learn something from your friend about skiing, but you will also learn something about teaching from the act of teaching your friend. Read a book. Do a computer search on something about which you wish to know more.

In post-modern 21st century life, continue to learn or you quickly become an anachronism. Do not wait for a lull in the action to spend time learning, but apply yourself to the process of learning something you find meaningful whenever you are frustrated, dispirited, or have more time to yourself than usual. Behave as if you are indulging yourself in something delicious and forbidden instead of thinking of the learning process as a survival skill.

Create Something

We have limited control over many things in our lives. Anyone in job search knows that after she has done everything within her power to do, the process shifts to being controlled by decision makers outside her. At such times, when you are waiting to see what might materialize in your career, materialize something for yourself through any form of creative expression that appeals to you.

You may not be known for your carpentry, gardening, writing, dancing, or oil painting skills and you may never make a living from them, but creative acts provide the opportunity to produce something tangible to be experienced through the senses. Therein lies one of the beautiful things about creative expression. When tangible results seem to be manifesting slowly in your career, and particularly when you are in waiting mode, creative self-expression can be a vehicle for manifesting the tangible.

In addition to manifesting something tangible, the very process of creating awakens internal powers that may have been asleep for some time. So much of what we do in life seems to overdevelop the rational thinking processes. While the creation of art, in all its forms, surely taps into the intellect, it also has the remarkable ability to bypass the intellect for a time, tapping into something primal, visceral, and symbolic. In doing so, a more holistic, more complete, expression of who the artist *is* finds expression. Surrendering to the flow of creative expression can create a subtle shift in the body and mind, making it easier to surrender to other life processes, as well.

Give Something Back

There is unity and oneness to everything in the Universe, but on an ongoing basis, you may be more conscious of the individual body in which you are enfleshed and the very personal life you live than that oneness. It is easy to become preoccupied with the details of one's own life, and in becoming preoccupied, lose perspective.

When your career feels stalled or progressing slowly, when it feels as if everything that could go wrong has gone wrong, or when you just feel uninspired, look outside yourself and the confines of your own life to find renewal. Begin by giving something back to the world.

Volunteer your talents and your time to an organization or an individual. Help build a hiking trail; teach an adult non-reader to read; collect and distribute donations for your favorite charity; cook or serve food at a soup kitchen for the homeless; or give encouragement to a fellow journeyer in the midst of career exploration or job search. It matters less what you do than that you do something selfless to benefit another.

Several things happen when you move your focus from your own life to the larger world around you:

- You are reminded of your connection to all beings and all things, of your essential oneness with everything else in the Universe.
- That reconnection with the oneness propels you into the energetic flow, the *zone*, in which all things can be created and all things are possible.
- Your action on behalf of others becomes a physical expression of gratitude for all the blessings life has bestowed upon you, a conscious return of the favors you have received. And, as it happens, gratitude is one of the most powerful generators of positive energy in the Universe.
- You honor one of the Universal Principles, that of maintaining the flow of giving and receiving. By doing so, you benefit yourself as well as others.
- Your perspective on, and gratitude for, what you already have grows exponentially.
- You feel uplifted by using your body and mind in service to others.

Ultimately, by giving something back to the world, you buoy up your spirits and gift yourself as much as those you help.

> Penelope was having a bad day, the kind of day that made her wish she had never left her bed. Early that morning she had received a call about a position for which she was a candidate, with a company for whom she very much wanted to work. While she had been a finalist for the position, they had chosen someone else for the job.

Telling herself that there was nothing to do but accept the situation and continue on, one foot in front of the other, she had then gone off to a professional meeting at which she was a scheduled speaker. The words to her speech seemed lifeless as they left her mouth and the audience seemed bored. By the time she left the meeting, she was ready to go home and crawl under the covers in her bed. But first, she needed food.

Penelope stopped at a food court and purchased a bowl of soup and roll to take home with her. It would serve as comfort food. As she stood at a light, waiting for the *walk* sign to appear, a homeless woman approached her. The woman asked for money, saying that she was hungry. Penelope reached for her purse, then realized she was *holding* a bag with nourishing food. She offered her lunch to the homeless woman, who seemed startled by the fact that a woman would so quickly offer her own lunch. She accepted the bag with a mumbled, "Thank you, and God bless."

With a sigh, Penelope returned to the food court vendor for another bowl of soup. The clerk looked as startled as the homeless woman and asked what had brought her back so quickly. Penelope explained that she had just given her soup to a homeless woman. The clerk served up another bowl of soup, bagged it, tossed in a warm roll, and handed the bag to Penelope. "It's on us," he said.

Somehow, Penelope thought, things seemed to be looking up.

Catch Yourself In The Act Of Talking Trash To Yourself

One of the most pervasive perversions in human experience is the human practice of diminishing, degrading, and denying the essential goodness of the self through the ongoing judgment of the internal critic. You *talk trash* to yourself:

- Every time you mentally create worst-case scenarios that have not yet happened;
- Every time you allow the internal critic to nag you about all of the not-good-enough things in your life;
- Every time you tell yourself that whatever someone else has that you do not have is just not fair;

- Every time you criticize yourself for mistakes made long ago that continue to haunt you;
- Every time you harangue yourself for not being perfect;
- Every time you question your essential worthiness; and
- Every time you even *hint* to yourself that your essential nature is not one of pure love.

Catch yourself in the act of talking trash to yourself. Much of this internal abuse goes unnoticed because it is almost constant; a deleterious internal whispering that is activated whenever the mind is not deliberately focused on everyday matters. The very act of alerting yourself to the possibility that you may be talking trash to yourself, frequently or occasionally, will program you to catch yourself in the act of doing it.

Once you catch yourself in the act, *choose again.* Change your mind, literally, by changing your thoughts. You cannot erase the moments of negative self-talk that passed through your mind last week or last year, but the present moment provides a fresh opportunity to change your mind, choose again, and begin to replace negative self-talk with encouraging and uplifting internal dialogue.

Become Friends With Yourself, At A Deep Level

Start now, right where you are, to begin to become friends with yourself at a deep level. We are all doing the best we can with the information and capabilities we currently have. *You* have already been doing the best you can. You would have already done better if you could. There is no need to wait until you are smarter, kinder, more skilled at relationships, or better in *any* way than you are at this moment. Begin, right now, to ease up on yourself. You are exactly as you should be in and for this moment. If you long to improve yourself as a human being, your chances of success will improve when you begin to accept and appreciate exactly who you are in this moment. If you tell yourself that you will be easier on yourself when you have achieved a measure of perfection, that very reluctance to accept who you are *now* will hamper your ability to perfect yourself.

Some of the most gifted and talented people I know are willing to accept that everyone else deserves a break because they are, after all human; but these same people frequently hold themselves to a much higher standard. It may feel humble to live this approach but it is, in fact, incredibly arrogant. You may *wish* to stand apart from the rest of the species but, sorry, you are also one of us, warts and all. You deserve to accept yourself to the same degree you are willing to accept others.

If you have done the work on accepting yourself recommended earlier in this book but continue to have problems with self-acceptance, take the work deeper. We all experience triggers that challenge the self-image and we all have multiple layers covering the deepest levels of self-doubt and self-deprecation. Work with these triggers to take the process into a deeper level of understanding and self-acceptance. Realize that this process is never truly complete, as long as you are in human form.

A Process For Digging Deeper

1. Take a deep breath, step back from your feelings, just a little, and open yourself to thoughts and feelings that may provide clues to whatever triggered your current state.

2. Did an *event* trigger thoughts and feelings? If an event served as a trigger, what memories arise as you think of the event? What thoughts and feelings are associated with the memories triggered by the event?

3. If an event did not serve as a trigger, allow your mind to return to whatever you were *doing or thinking* when you experienced the trigger. What were you doing? What were you thinking? What feelings are associated with the activity? Where do your thoughts take you?

4. Trace your thoughts and feelings back, through layers, as if peeling an onion. Each layer is valid and true. Each layer takes you to yet another layer until there are no further layers.

5. What sits at the core of your thoughts and feelings? What is the core layer of the onion you peel?
6. What sits in this layer, fundamental to your thoughts, feelings, and beliefs about yourself, which you recognize as lacking in self-acceptance, lacking in respect for who and what you are *in this moment*?
7. What do you choose, in this moment, as your basic understanding of yourself, as your personal truth? Step into that truth.

Realize that so long as you are enfleshed in human form, there will probably be layers of understanding to work through. Celebrate each understanding that takes you into a deeper acceptance of yourself.

Don't Just Sit There, Intuit Something!

When everything seems to be falling apart, it is useful to thank the rational-logical mind (left brain) for everything it has been doing on your behalf, ask it to relax for a while, and invoke the power of the holistic, intuitive (right brain) side of you.

Just as your intuition, in the form of your internal guidance system, was useful to you when the destination was unclear, it is a resource of vast assistance when you have days or weeks during which the very fabric of your life seems to be coming apart at the seams.

When everything is problematic, and nothing you thought you knew is helping the situation, it may be helpful to ask the following question:

If I knew what would help, what would that be?

This is a subtle and powerful mind manipulation designed to access your intuition. Your rational mind does not have an answer. Your intuitive self may, however, know just what is needed to return you to balance and harmony. Allow your intuitive self to offer answers.

Are You Feeling Envy?

What you envy in the life and accomplishments of another may be what *you* are capable of and desire for yourself but have not yet manifested in your life. Your feelings of envy can be a postcard to you from your Higher Self telling you to pay attention because that which you envy may be a part of your own possible future. If you ignore that postcard from your Higher Self, you miss an opportunity to wake up, recognize what is possible, and take steps towards it. If you read that postcard with care, you may begin to shift your view of yourself, take actions towards a different possible future, and more fully hum to the spin of your internal gyroscope.

Return To Beginner's Mind

Human beings, when caught up in human doing, have an amazing ability to complicate matters. When the *doing* part of life is not working the way you would like, you may become caught up in the drama of analyzing what is not working. You may, in fact, analyze the situation to the point of short-circuiting your system. When you short-circuit the system, the intuitive process shuts down, suppressing your ability to experience the present moment.

At such times, the most useful thing one can do is to return to beginner's mind.

Beginner's Mind
(Also Found On Accompanying CD)

1. Sit comfortably straight in a chair. Take two or three deep breaths and allow your body to relax and become as comfortable as you choose to be. Feel your feet on the floor and their connection with Mother

Earth. Experience the groundedness that She provides.

2.   Imagine you are in bed, slowly awakening from a refreshing night of sleep. You feel warmth on your face and as you slowly open your eyes, you see a thin stream of light flowing in from a small opening between the mostly-closed curtains that cover a window.

3.   You lie in bed, perfectly comfortable and at peace. The warmth from the sun on your face feels pleasant and the room, mostly in shadows, is peaceful. As you slowly awaken, you are aware of a dream you were having when the sunlight awakened you. The dream is gone now, but a luscious remnant of it remains, filling you with delicious promise.

4.   You move to arise and as your feet meet the floor and you raise your body, you look about the room. This room is in a small inn, one you stopped at the night before when you were weary and needed rest. You have come to this place by choice and need. You have not been here before and, as you slowly get your bearings, you wonder what it holds for you.

5.   You walk to the window. The draperies are richly textured and woven through with golden threads. They are so long that they puddle at the floor and the sight of them provides an interesting sense of comfort.

6.   You push aside the draperies to look outside. You are struck by what you see and unlatch the window to get a better look outside and to smell the new day. As the window opens, your nose is filled with the rich smell of flowers and herbs. You realize that this scent is a thrilling combination of the plants you see outside the window in the garden below. You smell rose, lavender, sage, and a mingling of other scents.

7.   The garden is stunning. As your eyes take it in, you see the luxury of this beautiful, lovingly tended place and have the strange sensation that you have come home. The chirping of birds meets your ears and there is the buzzing sound of bees feeding at the delicate centers of flowers. The sounds are as satisfying as the sights. You feel as First Man or First Woman must have felt on the first day of the world. You experience a wonderful sense of positive anticipation. You have no

idea what awaits you this day, but you know, deep within you, that whatever it holds will be completely satisfying to you.

8. You turn from the window to look at your room. It is comfortably appointed with everything you need. In fact, it is more than comfortable. Everything in it is beautiful and pleases you as it would if you had arranged it yourself, to fulfill your fantasies of what a room should be.

9. You run your hand across the rich wood of a dresser. It feels silky to the touch and you think to yourself that you have never felt such pleasure in touching wood. In fact, you wonder if you have ever before bothered to appreciate the feel of wood at all.

10. You notice a bowl of fruit on a small table near the window. You are surprised to see that the bowl is filled with all your favorite fruits and you wonder how the innkeeper could have known exactly what would please you. His thoughtfulness touches you. You pick up the bowl and bring your nose to the fruit. There is the smell of perfection to it. The fruit has been picked at its height, just for you. You select a piece that does not require peeling, feel the firm ripeness to it, and take a bite. You think that while you have eaten fruit many times, it has never tasted so wonderful. You taste this piece of fruit as if tasting fruit for the first time. It is completely satisfying.

11. In the swell of sensations, you have forgotten for a moment just why you are here. You know there is purpose to it but, somehow, the purpose is secondary to the pure, raw pleasure of experiencing this new day in this familiar body that also feels new.

12. As you finish the delicious piece of fruit, you turn to see your travel bag sitting next to the bed. You are surprised to find that, lying atop it is a set of clothes, waiting for you. They may be yours, but you cannot quite recall wearing them before. Like everything else around you, they are beautiful, feel wonderful to the touch, appear comfortable, and seem completely appropriate for whatever you choose to do.

13. You bathe and otherwise attend to your morning ritual, experiencing

even these simple activities in a new way because you are in a place that is both simple and luxurious, perfect for your needs and surprisingly beautiful. You attire yourself in the clothes that have been sitting out, waiting for you, and you look at the door to your room.

14. You think to yourself that you have no idea what the day will bring, let alone where your journey may take you, but you have a sense of positive anticipation about discovering what awaits you.

15. You realize that you are experiencing beginner's mind and set your intent to bring this mindset forward, into every area of your life.

16. When you are ready, return to ordinary consciousness, carrying with you the perfect sense of beginner's mind.

Are You Transforming?

Transformation is uncomfortable, disconcerting, unsettling, and necessary in life. If you are wandering around your home feeling as if you have finally awakened after a long sleep, congratulations! You may be in the throws of transformation.

If so, you may be unsure of where you are or what to do next. You may experience hours or days of dark night of the soul, followed by hours or days of pure bliss. You may sense that you have been, somehow, stripped right down to your bones or you may feel that you have died and are only beginning to feel the stirrings of rebirth within you. The experience may be one of being in uncharted territory, on the high seas in a small boat. If you are lucky, you may realize that, high above you, is a star to guide you.

You may look into your closet and wonder how you could have ever been satisfied wearing anything in it or you may suddenly decide to change your hairstyle. You may find yourself drawn to try foods you have shunned in the past. You may take up a new sport or creative pursuit.

However you experience transformation, understand that the butterfly in its pupa state, within its chrysalis, does not emerge without struggling a bit to free itself. Its struggle, shared by every other butterfly in the same state, is, nonetheless, unique and must be experienced alone.

Be gentle with yourself. Treat body, mind, spirit, and emotions with respect and care. Do not resist the process, but also do not try to rush it. Accept the process, and its unique timing, as your being's movement towards growth—because that is exactly what it is.

Marguerite sits before a comforting fire on a cold winter evening. A warm shawl around her shoulders, she is lost in thought about all the things that have brought her to this winter night and the peace she feels within. She thinks back to the beginning of her apprenticeship with the shaman Awakens Many Spirits, several years earlier. A synchronous series of events had brought her to him and she had known, from the first look into the depths of his brown eyes, that she was meant to know him.

When Awakens Many Spirits had accepted her as apprentice, he had told her that her life would change. It had seemed a simple thing to say. Marguerite had spent the year before that first meeting in the process of rewriting her life. She felt that nothing in the apprenticeship could be more profound than what she had was experiencing on her own.

She was wrong. Now, years later, Marguerite smiles to the fire, the room, the night, and to herself. She had been an innocent when she began that apprenticeship. Her life *had* changed. It had, in fact, transformed. Had she realized the depth and breadth of those changes to come when she began her apprenticeship, she would surely have doubted that she would have the strength needed. She suspects that she also surely would have plunged into the apprenticeship anyway. She knew, even then, that when destiny knocks, it is a good idea to answer the door.

The early months, the entire first year in fact, had been difficult. Strange new things had awakened in Marguerite, new skills and abilities, visions, dreams, and a strength of intent that had surprised her. At the same time, Marguerite had found herself spontaneously recapitulating her life, in bits and pieces, on an ongoing basis. Each episode of recapitulation had been profound and unsettling, but each had also led to a deeper, wider understanding and appreciation of herself.

More than once, Marguerite had contacted Awakens Many Spirits to ask a single question, "What is *happening* to me?"

With different words for different contacts, Awakens Many Spirits always gave the same answer, "You are transforming."

Now, having successfully completed her apprenticeship, Marguerite thinks of Awakens Many Spirits with great fondness and respect. He had guided her simply and with few words, but he had always gently led her back to herself and the process of her transformation. Marguerite now walked her own shamanic path. She served her community. She practiced the old healing rituals. She performed ceremony. Her life had changed completely, had transformed. Sitting before her fire this cold winter evening, Marguerite smiles to herself once again. Life is good for her and she is grateful that the gods had not shared *too* much of her future with her during those days of apprenticeship.

Sometimes the most important thing to do when destiny knocks is to just answer the door, without over-thinking what destiny carries into your home.

Surrendering To The Journey

The suggestions offered in this chapter began with considering that Divine timing may be at play and ended with contemplating the possibility that you may be in the throws of an important transformation. Allowing for the possibility of either—or both—of these suggestions requires that you surrender to the journey, itself. In the final analysis, it is your willingness to surrender to the journey that will allow you to accept the days, weeks, or months when some or all aspects of it seem more challenging than you would like. If mother told you there would be days like this, she probably also told you that the way you navigate those days will define your mettle as a human being. Welcome it all, even the troublesome parts, because it is all part of the gift of life.

Chapter 11

THE JOB OFFER

*First, breathe. With every inspiration of air,
you allow for greater internal inspiration
about the proper response to the offer.*

A t the end of a long journey, the world traveler finds herself with an offer for a new journey. She may be weary from the journey that now draws to a close, but she is thrilled with this new opportunity. She wants to give a loud and enthusiastic "Yes!" to the offer. She is very close to doing this when some part of her rises up. She remembers to breathe and she begins to listen with both her physical ears and her inner ears.

The career exploration/job search journeyer will also receive an offer after days, weeks, or months of dreaming, fantasizing, and planning for this moment. She may also want to call out, "Yes!" Wisdom, however, would ask her to do something else.

First, Breathe

With every inspiration of air, you allow for a greater internal inspiration about the proper response to the offer. Allow yourself a few breaths, and then…listen. Let your immediate *internal* response to the offer be one of slightly detached interest. Allow your immediate *external* response be one of allowing the organization's representative to provide details about the offer: the job itself, the title, the pay, the benefits, and the perquisites. Ask questions if you are unclear about any aspect of the offer. Be clear that you would like to see the offer in writing.

Then…Still Refrain From Calling Out "Yes!"

It is important to let the organization's representative know you are appreciative of the offer and very interested in the organization. It is also important to tell him that you want to consider the offer carefully. Whether this is the offer of a lifetime or an offer you are unsure you want to accept, be enthusiastic. The organization has probably spent many weeks searching for the perfect candidate and they have concluded that *you* are this perfect candidate. Have respect for that.

Have respect for yourself, too. You may have been in job search long enough to wonder if you will ever be employed again. Or this offer may have materialized with no direct effort on your part, during a time when you thought your current creative engagement was just fine. Either way, *any* offer of employment deserves careful consideration. Breathe, listen, get answers to your questions, and be enthusiastic. Tell the organization's representative that you want to give the offer careful consideration and that you will require some time to think it over and talk it over with your family (and/or advisors).

Many people are afraid to do this. They fear the offer, if not accepted immediately, may dematerialize as quickly as it materialized. In fact, this is highly unlikely. The organization *wants* you and has gone to no little time and expense to *find* you. Most organizations will expect you to step back and give it some thought, even if they are just as anxious for you to say, "Yes!" as *you* are to say it.

Understand that this is not manipulation or subterfuge on your part. It is not a way to coerce the organization to increase its offer. You *may* ultimately ask for more money, but that is not the point. The purpose for delay is to ask both your rational-logical thinking side and your internal guidance system for help in making a decision that is good for *you* at this time. Most organizations have come to appreciate and accept this as a part of the process. The enlightened organization will *want* you to take this time, knowing that the best employees come to them through a process that is both magical and well reasoned out.

How Much Time Should You Take To Consider The Offer?

How much time should you take to consider the offer? Actually, that depends on a number of things: how quickly you get the offer in writing, how many details need to be clarified and/or negotiated, your ability to get the counsel of your advisors, and how clear you are about whether or not to accept. You may want to take a couple of days to consider the offer, before the first negotiations take place, if negotiations are in order. Do not delay the process unnecessarily. It should not take a week for you to decide if this creative engagement, in the form of a job, is for you—providing you can negotiate the details.

Then What?

What should you do immediately after completing your conversation with the person who has made the offer? First, congratulate yourself. Next, notify your family and your coach, if you have one. Regardless how good you are at sorting through complex business transactions or how good you are at negotiating offers, this is definitely the time for careful consideration with the benefit of counsel from those, like your family, who are affected by the decision and those, like your career coach, who have facilitated and guided you through the journey.

Considerations

What kinds of things should you consider in making your decision?

- First and foremost, ask yourself if this position meets or approaches your criterion for the *ideal* job?
  - ✦ Does it represent a new and different ideal, if not the version you have envisioned?
  - ✦ Is it a step along the path to the ideal job?

The ideal is to accept an offer for some version of the *ideal* job. It is curious, however, how often the Universe sends us something we had not previously considered to be ideal, but find, once in the experience, that it is even better than anything we could have conjured with our own minds. Do not abandon what is right and good for you, but do leave room for the delightful possibility that the Universe may know what is perfect for you even better than you do.

- If not your ideal, or something that points the way to your ideal, how does this opportunity stand in relation to your needs at the present time? Sometimes the ideal needs to be deferred for a time because your bank balance is speaking to you in a loud and harsh voice. There is something quite honorable about a person who will do whatever it takes (preferably legal and socially acceptable) to pay the bills and take care of herself and her family. Consider your personal circumstances in making your decision.
- Have you done your homework relating to the organization?
  - ✦ Have you researched it through the Internet, your investment broker, friends and acquaintances who work there, and in every other practical way?
  - ✦ Are you happy with what you have learned? Are any of your boundaries (geographic, cultural, financial, or any others) not in keeping with this offer?
- Is the compensation offered, both in terms of base pay and all other

forms of compensation, in keeping with your needs and expectations, as well as in keeping with the market and the talents and experience you bring to the job?

- Are the benefits equal to or better than those at your current or last job?
  - ✦ What medical benefits are offered? Is there a 401K plan and is there a stock option or phantom stock program? If so, are they equal or better than the programs you will be leaving or have left?
  - ✦ Are you being offered equity in the company?
  - ✦ Are you being made an offer that keeps you whole in vacation and holiday time or even exceeds the vacation and holiday time provided by your last job?
  - ✦ Is there a tuition reimbursement program?
  - ✦ Is there an adoption assistance program?
  - ✦ Does the organization provide either paid or unpaid sabbaticals, based upon length of service or some other criterion?
  - ✦ Are there other benefits or perquisites that are important to you and are they a part of the offer?
- If you are considering an offer for an executive level position (Senior Management Team, usually Vice President or above) does the offer outline provisions for your separation, should the organization change in ownership, your position be eliminated, or there is mutual agreement that the relationship is not working? Such provisions should include, at a minimum, those for separation pay and a period of medical benefit continuation.
- Are you clear about your job responsibilities, your place in the organization, the chain of command reporting to you and through whom you report, your title, and the process for developmental and promotional opportunities? Does the position allow for or require travel and, if so, are you clear about the travel requirements? Are travel requirements acceptable to you?
- When does the organization want you to begin your employment? Does this timing work for you?

- What does your internal guidance system have to say about the offer? Earlier in the book, I gave you a process for determining an internal *yes* and an internal *no*. This has, hopefully, been a useful tool for you throughout the journey: with networking opportunities, the marketing effort, interviews, and in countless other ways. It is particularly helpful at this time.

  + Take the time to do an internal check to see if the opportunity being offered elicits a *yes* or a *no* from your internal guidance system.

  + Then, dig deeper. If you get a *yes*, ask if there are issues you need to consider before giving your answer. If so, do some internal checking to discern what they might be.

  + If you get a *no*, ask if there is any refinement to the offer that will make it acceptable to your internal guidance system or, if not, ask if there is another opportunity at this organization that may be suitable. If you continue to get a *no*, ask for guidance on the meaning of being made this offer at this time. Sometimes there is meaning as great in a *no* as in a *yes*.

- How does your immediate family feel about the offer? What guidance does your career coach have?

Negotiating The Offer

Assuming that your rational-logical thinking processes and your internal guidance system provide encouragement for you to accept an offer, and assuming that every other piece of input important to you leans in the direction of accepting, consider the offer from the standpoint of what will inspire you to accept it and what will be a deal breaker. Your coach can be invaluable in helping you at this point in the process. S/he may raise considerations you had not postulated, may encourage you to ask for that which you are afraid to ask, and may be the voice of reason if you become over-zealous in negotiating.

This *is* the time to negotiate. There is no better time. The organization wants you and you have leverage now, before you take the position, which you may never again have with this organization.

I am suggesting that this is a time for negotiation, not a time to become carried away with greed. This is not about winning, but about fairness to both parties. If I thought it would be understood and accepted within organizations, I would suggest that where pay is concerned you ask the organization for the absolute most they can reasonably and fairly offer...and not a penny more. In that way, you would be assured of a fair offer. I have actually suggested this approach to a client or two, though I think it impractical in most cases.

Your negotiations need to be based on what is necessary and fair, what motivates you to accept the offer, and what will kill the deal if not met. Only you, with a little help from family and coach, can determine that.

Look at the offer in its totality. What is less than inspiring about it or missing from it? What is *really* important to you? Negotiating pay may be the critical issue for some people, while negotiating benefits, title, or time off may be critical for someone else. *All* of these may be critical to you where your current situation and this particular offer are concerned. Is there a component to the offer that will be a deal breaker for you if not addressed? If there is, you *must* consider negotiating it because your acceptance hinges upon it.

Employers and candidates sometimes mistrust one another unnecessarily. In my experience, most employers are honorable, as are most candidates. Negotiating the offer need not be a win-lose game, steeped in devious and dubious machinations and ending with one party feeling good and the other feeling bad. The best creative engagements are entered into when two parties, each respecting and honoring the other, want what is good for both. To negotiate well is to discuss, compromise where needed, and come to some agreement that benefits both parties beautifully. Do not settle for something less than this. You have come too far on your journey to accept what will not work for you or demand what will not work for the other.

Before you begin your negotiations, remind yourself that you and the other party are linked. At some level, the two of you are one—because everything and everyone in the deep, wide Universe *is* one at the deepest level. If you bring harm to another, you bring harm to yourself. If you allow another to bring harm to you, you allow them to bring harm to themselves, too. Proceed with honor.

More candidates fail to negotiate on their own behalf, at least without encouragement, than attempt to negotiate in an unreasonable manner. For this reason, seeking the counsel of your coach, a respected friend, or anyone else skilled in artful and honorable negotiating is not simply helpful, but probably necessary. If you are working with a coach, the job offer and its negotiation are probably high fun for him/her. It is extremely satisfying to assist a client in the career coaching equivalent to a novel's denouement.

Negotiations need to last long enough to accomplish what is important and not so long that both parties begin to wonder if this is really a relationship made in heaven. It is impossible to say more than this. Every negotiation is different. In most cases, however, my work with clients has involved negotiations lasting from a day to a week, seldom more than that.

One last bit of advice about negotiating: negotiate your start date to allow you some time to revel in your good fortune. It is common for organizations to want the newly hired to start immediately or, at the very least, at the soonest possible time, as dictated by candidate notice giving to current employers and corporate orientation schedules. This is understandable, but it ignores the possibility for the candidate having one of the best times of his or her life. There is *nothing* like the time between offer acceptance and start date. There will be few, maybe no, days in your life as sweet and free from mundane concerns as those during this time and if you choose to take a brief vacation at this time, you will probably find it to be one of the best vacations you have ever had. Life provides rare opportunities for gleeful freedom from care. The time between offer acceptance and start date can be one of them. Take advantage of it and realize that you deserve this reward for a journey well taken!

What If The Opportunity Is Not Right For You?

There is no glory—and no benefit to your career—in accepting an offer that is wrong for you. You may have been in search for the perfect opportunity for a long time. You may be weary from the journey. You may *want* the offer and the opportunity to be perfect. But have the courage to walk away from it if it is not right for you.

If your internal guidance system, coupled with your rational-logical thinking processes, gives you a *no*, consider walking away. If the boundaries you set for yourself are still valid, and they are violated seriously by the opportunity or offer, consider walking away. If you cannot negotiate past some part of the offer that is a deal breaker, consider walking away. If there are too many questions left unanswered in the negotiations, the negotiations have been decidedly one-sided in favor of the organization, and you feel unsettled and uncomfortable about the organization, consider walking away. If nothing is right about the company or the offer and you are just desperate to leave your current job, consider walking away. If the opportunity seriously takes you off a path for which you feel passion, consider walking away.

Take enough time to sense whether what you are experiencing is (1) merely stage fright, or (2) your internal guidance system alerting you that accepting the offer will truly be the wrong choice for you. If it is the wrong choice, your career, your bank balance, and your sense of self will not be served by trying to convince yourself that it is a good choice. Know *when* to walk away and have the *courage* to walk away when it is time to do so. You are the only one who will know when that is and you are the only one who can summon the courage to walk away.

Jobs opportunities had always come to Mary with little effort on her part. For the first dozen years of her career, this worked well for her. Then, just as she was beginning to take a serious look at what she really *wanted* in a career, Mary was one of many to lose her job in a corporate downsizing.

Bright, organized and efficient, Mary made good use of the first few weeks of job search. She revised her résumé and explored the possibilities. Already the consummate networker, Mary scheduled a series of lunches and drinks with colleagues, knowing that her next position was more likely to be found through vigorous networking than in any other way.

Mary's networking netted results quickly. She was offered a position with a company she knew little about, but she was anxious enough to get back to work that she accepted it without either researching the company or checking with her internal guidance system about it. In fact, Mary's career had evolved so effortlessly in the past that she was completely unpracticed at conferring with her internal guidance system where career was concerned.

It only took a couple of months for Mary to realize she had made a mistake in accepting the position. She was miserable. The work involved far more cold calling than she had been led to expect and there was little in the way of guidance from her superiors. She quit, believing that one mistake in many years of work was nothing with which to be concerned.

Again, Mary's investment in networking paid great dividends. This time, she accepted a position working for someone she knew, a vendor to one of the companies for whom she had previously worked. Again, Mary accepted the position quickly and with little internal or external research about the opportunity. What Mary expected to be a fun job was not. She found her boss to be emotionally volatile and demanding.

Before Mary had accepted this new position, a wise friend had urged her to determine whether this was the right job for her by researching the opportunity thoroughly...and allowing her intuition to guide her. Mary realized, as she reeled from the effects of her mistake, that her friend had been right.

Mary quit this job, too. But *this* time she began to practice the fine art of listening to the small, still voice within. When the next opportunity came, Mary did the appropriate research on the company *and* allowed her internal guidance system to advise her. A year later, she believes that she has the world's best job!

If you have determined that it is the moment to walk away and summon the courage to do so, it will be, in shamanic terms, an act of power. Acts of power have a tendency to serve as beacons and magnets for what has the possibility of serving you, and the world, more beautifully and perfectly than what was possible before the act of power. If this is not the right opportunity for you, allow it to pass away. A better opportunity, one more perfectly suited to you, will likely find its way to you.

> Kathy had been in search for several months and had, in fact, begun work to identify the perfect opportunity for her before leaving her last position. She worked in a highly specialized field, which meant that job opportunities were a national, not a local or regional, search for her.
>
> Kathy had thoroughly examined her life, her career, her calling, and her opportunities. She had pursued her search with vigor. Finally, she found an intriguing opportunity in another state. After successfully passing through the preliminary stages of the hiring process, Kathy was invited to interview with the company at its corporate headquarters. She prepared for the interview process with the same vigor she had brought to the search phase. The interviews went well. In fact, she was offered the position.
>
> Something did not feel right about the opportunity to Kathy. It was a good company and a good opportunity. She was a bit perplexed about her concern. Still, she could not shake the feeling that this was not the job for her. After giving the opportunity due consideration, Kathy rejected the offer.
>
> A couple of months later, another company asked Kathy to interview for what she considered her ideal job. The opportunity was truly magical. She flew to Chicago for her interviews with a special sense of rightness about the opportunity. Not only did the interviews go well, but she felt as comfortable with this opportunity as she had felt uncomfortable with the previous one.
>
> After consulting with her coach and negotiating the offer, she accepted with a joyous heart and optimism for her future.

Notify Your Network

Many people have likely assisted you on your journey and you have probably added a number of people to your network during the journey. It is important to thank those who have helped you and to notify your entire network of your new work home. The best time to prepare this announcement, whether you plan to deliver it through e-mail or snail mail, is *before* you start the new job.

Once you have begun your new creative engagement, you will be swept up in meeting new people, learning the job, and allowing yourself to shine, thereby reminding the employer of how smart the organization was to hire you. Despite your best intentions, you will find you have little time to draft and send out a notice to your network. Prepare it now, before you begin, while you have the time. Thank your supporters and provide contact information: the name of the organization, your title, address, and phone/e-mail information if you have it. The letter need not be long, but it needs to express gratitude to those who helped and supported you on your journey and it needs to reflect your enthusiasm about the new creative engagement.

If you would like to send out notice by mail, make an effort to get company stationery to print it on. This is not only a classy thing to do (and economical), but also sends a clear message of connection to and allegiance with the new employer. Most employers will happily provide you with as much organization letterhead as you will need, along with matching envelopes.

Whether you prepare a letter or an e-mail, you need not send it out before you begin your new job. In fact, it is a good idea to wait at least until your first day to send out the notice. Let this be your first official act the first day on the job!

Celebrate Your Success

The very fact that you have been made an offer is, itself, a cause for celebration. Celebrate. If you decline an offer because it is not right for you, celebrate the offer and celebrate both your wisdom and courage in declining it. If the offer is perfect, accept it and...celebrate. Congratulations!

Chapter 12

THE PERFECT JOB IS YOURS. NOW WHAT?

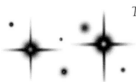

The Grail question may be one of the most important questions for you to ask periodically throughout your career. Whom does the Grail serve?

The journey has ended. It has been a journey the world traveler will remember for a long time, perhaps to the end of his days. Our world traveler is at home, happy and secure. He spends time reacquainting himself with his home turf and he attends to his household, ensuring that it meets his needs and serves him well. But he also wants to be ready for the next journey, realizing that there will always be another journey. The journeyer may put away his gear, but he knows exactly where it is stored and he will keep his passport up to date, ready for the next opportunity to travel. He may begin to think about where he would like to travel next. He may even begin to collect brochures and books about far away places that hold interest to him.

The career exploration/job search journeyer also needs to attend to his environment, once he has landed in the perfect job...for now. He needs to be prepared for the next career exploration/job search journey because there will likely be one, perhaps after a long and happy engagement, perhaps sooner. What can he do to maintain his professional edge and prepare for the journey to come?

Keep Your Passport Current

You may be so familiar with your résumé by now that, like some fine friends with whom you have spent many intimate hours and have become overly familiar, you are now ready to put it aside for a time. That is understandable, but do not set it aside for long. Just as you need to keep your passport current because you never know when an enticing opportunity to travel overseas may come your way, you need to keep your résumé current because you may be faced with the opportunity for *the next* perfect job at any time.

Take the time to add your new job to your résumé soon after you begin. You will not have metrics and accomplishments at that point, but it will be a start. Then collect the metrics you need to make it meaningful. It may take a few months to acquire compelling accomplishments to add to it, but be sure to make note of those accomplishments, as you achieve them, and revise your résumé periodically, to reflect them.

Maintain, Expand, And Cultivate Your Network

If you thought that networking could be put aside when the perfect creative engagement was secured, you are wrong. Networking is a vital part of maintaining your professional edge. Your focus may change when you have a job/career you love, but networking is still critical. Why?

- You may have the job you love now, but with the lightning speed at which organizations change in the 21st century, the job could evaporate by the time the sun comes up tomorrow morning. A job is no longer a lifelong thing. Do not fret about what might happen, but do realize that the network you have worked so hard to create needs to be maintained. You may need to press it into service at any time.
- Organizations have a tendency to become incredibly inbred. Just

as inbreeding weakens a species, it also weakens organizations. Networking will help you keep a fresh mindset about the world, particularly if your network is richly infused with a diversity of people and thinking. Like a powerful shot of vitamins, that fresh mindset can be injected into your organization as you go about problem solving and creating.

- No one can know everything. If you have kept in touch with your network, they will welcome your calls when you need to brainstorm or look for best practices.
- No one likes to be used. An important part of attending to your network involves giving something back to the people who have been generous to you. *You* need to be there for *them*, too. The person who calls only when she is in job search will find that, over time, fewer and fewer of her calls get returned…and one definition of power is having your calls returned.

This Is Not The Time To Abandon Professional Organizations

Whether you are in the for-profit or not-for-profit sector, employers are notorious for demanding just about everything their employees are willing to give. Long hours are standard. When the demands pile up, it is easy to find time by abandoning professional organization membership or, even if you maintain the membership, by going into inactive mode. This is a bad idea. Not only are professional organizations important to your commitment to maintain your network, they can:

- Help you keep your professional skills up to date;
- Be a place to test out new ideas;
- Be a haven, a place where you do not have to explain words or practices common to your profession; and
- an opportunity to develop and practice leadership skills if you are willing to commit to active involvement with the group.

Differentiate Yourself

Differentiating yourself was important in the job search. It is equally important if you want to keep the job you worked so hard to get. How do you do this?

- Keep showing up. It may be a sad statement about the quality of work being done in the Western world, but one of the easiest ways to differentiate yourself is to show up—today, tomorrow, every day. Showing up is more than bringing your body to work. It involves bringing your energy, your mind, your creativity, and your passion along with you.

- Keep service in mind. Despite the smoke and mirrors of competitive recruiting, the organization is not in the business to serve you, though enlightened organizations *do* value, honor, and serve their employees. You, on the other hand, have been hired to serve the organization. You can differentiate yourself by maintaining a service mindset and giving wide berth to those who want to know what the organization has done for *them* lately.

- Stay genuine. There is nothing more refreshing than the genuine article, the person without an agenda who is right out there, being her genuine self. This does not mean that you should risk crudeness or political ineptness. It does mean that you hold true to the unpretentious you and that you refrain from dramatically changing your demeanor or style to fit each person or group with which you interact.

- Keep learning. Do not just sit back and expect the organization to plan and sponsor your development. While many fine organizations have tuition reimbursement programs and pay for seminars, your personal development does not take place through a series of training events. It is an ongoing process and you are the primary orchestrator of it. Make your curiosity and thirst for learning something for which you are known.

- Demonstrate initiative and flexibility. Volunteer for assignments. Be willing to leave your comfort zone and enter uncharted territory. A friend (and former boss) of mine became an expert in every human resource discipline. As Vice President of Human Resources for a large company, he then volunteered to take leadership over the facilities department and the corporate administrative group. Once he had mastered these, he decided to leave the relative comfort of his, now broadened, human resource career and accepted a position in manufacturing operations within the same company. Now *that* is differentiating yourself!

- Monitor your organizational accomplishments and be willing to leverage them. While you might like to think that your boss and your boss's boss are keeping a running list of everything you have done for the organization, that is likely not the case. *You* need to be doing this and you need to (appropriately, please) use it to differentiate yourself.

Remember That Relationships Are What Keep… And Lose…Jobs

You are not in an isolation chamber. You are working with other human beings. The customers, the vendors, your peers, and your boss are human beings. Reminding yourself of this may save you a great deal of grief. I have seen the technically superior choke professionally, and even lose jobs, because they failed to nurture relationships.

Acknowledging relationships is not about sacrificing your true self. On the contrary, it is about being your full and true self *in relationship with other human beings*. With rare exceptions, we do not work alone. Hiring decisions are based, among other things, on a visceral sense of positive energy emanating from another human being. In other words, after all the sound, solid, and professionally defensible hiring practices have been honored, most employers still usually hire someone they *like*. Decisions about who stays and who goes in tough times are frequently made the same way: based on both professional contribution and who is a team player.

Organizations Want To Keep You As An Employee Until They Don't

There was a time when a person could hire on as a factory worker with a company two miles from home and stay with that company until he retired forty or more years later. It is true that, even today, organizations work hard to minimize turnover, but the climate has changed. As I said earlier, a job is no longer guaranteed for life. Organizations still may try to garner your loyalty and good organizations will deserve some of it. But do not assume that the loyalty any organization wants from you is necessarily going to be reciprocated. When times get tough, humans are sacrificed by organizations.

Maintain healthy boundaries. Your employer is not your father, brother, or best friend. Your employer, whether the company has two employees or two thousand employees, is in business (and that goes for the governmental and not-for-profit sectors as much as the for-profit sector). You are there to contribute to the organization's success and even though you may be the best in the company at what you do, the employment relationship can end at any time.

> Douglas accepted a full-time position with a software company for whom he had been doing consulting for some time. He liked the company and he liked the work. The job was demanding. Over the course of his first three months with the organization, he worked 16-18 hours a day, averaging 110 hours a week. He was good at his job and a dedicated, loyal employee.
>
> Five days before Christmas, the company announced that it was laying off over 50% of the workforce. Douglas was one of them. He was given less than two hours to vacate his office, which held, quite literally, a pickup truck load of equipment and other personal belongings. He struggled to get

his possessions to his apartment without the benefit of a pickup truck or any other vehicle during, as the fates would have it, one of the worst snowstorms in the history of the state of Wisconsin. The organization had provided his apartment and he had 72 hours to vacate it.

If dedication and being good at what you do can save your job, Douglas's job surely would have been saved. But a few days before Christmas, he found himself in a rental truck, fighting holiday traffic, as he moved himself and his possessions back home, a thousand miles or more away from the company for which he had worked day and night only a couple of days earlier.

Not every story is this dramatic, but there are many stories not so different from this one. Maintain healthy boundaries between you and your employer. Realize that the relationship is a business relationship, not a familial one. Give your best while remembering that this creative engagement may end at some point.

Know Thy Competitors

Know who the players are in your field and industry, those who compete for your organization's dollars. Who are they and what do they have to offer? Not only is knowing this important to maintaining your professional edge within your organization, it may be important should you decide to leave. Your organization's competitor just might be your next employer.

Keep Your Life Simple

The accoutrements of wealth are extremely seductive, but they are like the sirens of Greek mythology, which lured many a sailor to his death. It is tempting to complicate our lives with every pay increase: bigger houses; new cars; toys of both high and low tech variety; more entertainment to help us unwind; meals out because we think we do not have time to cook; designer clothing to keep our images intact; and every other trapping of the hip, young, affluent professional—whether or not we are actually hip, young, affluent, or professional.

It is extremely tempting to create a lifestyle that keeps pace with, and even outstrips, every pay increase. There is nothing wrong with enjoying the fruits of one's labor. There *is* something wrong with mindlessly complicating your life with financial obligations before you have created any kind of contingency plan or safety net and before you have thought about what adds real value to your life, as opposed to adding long-term obligation for ephemeral pleasure.

Keep it simple. Do not complicate your life to the point of creating a trap or prison for yourself. Every time there is a major economic downturn, those who have only expected an upward spiral and have only experienced increasing abundance have been startled and even devastated when *they* are part of an organization's downsizing or cut-back. If you live from paycheck to paycheck, have high balances on one or more credit cards, and never seem to get ahead of those things because you further complicate your life by adding financial obligations with every addition to your income, step back and give some thought to what might happen if your income evaporated for a week, a month, or a year.

Begin to set aside for the glorious or gruesome possibilities. Be extremely *self*-centered about this. Have something set aside should you wish, some day, to quit a job without having the next one waiting. Have something set aside for the possibility that you could someday lose a job suddenly. The next perfect job will not come to you easily if you are in a panic about your finances. You risk accepting what is not perfect for you because you are desperate. Prepare so you can give yourself some breathing room. Prepare so you will be able to deflect what is not perfect for you and attract what is.

Every time you avoid piling on life complications in the form of frivolous financial obligations, you buy yourself another little bit of freedom, and freedom is a beautiful thing. Having prepared enough to be free to quit what is no longer right for you is a heady experience. Having prepared enough to have the time to let yourself and the next perfect job find each other is more than just a heady experience, it is smart professional behavior. *Who you are* will always attract what is perfect for you more than *what you own.*

Know When A New Calling Has Arrived
Or When It Is Time To Move On

Life is about change. The work that inspired you a year ago…or two, or five, or ten…may not be what inspires you now. Attend to major shifts in what inspires and calls you in your work, in what you view as your purpose in life. For some, this is established at a young age and remains consistent throughout life. For others, it changes with life experience and growth, not so much because the earlier calling was mistaken, but as a matter of what might be called life purpose growth. If you stay stuck on what was once meaningful and purposeful for you, refusing to attend to the urgings of a new calling, you may become stale and dissatisfied with your work.

Likewise, attend to the political, cultural, and financial shifts within the organization in which your current perfect job resides. The energy of an organization can change, just as the energy of a person can change. Attend to the energetic changes that alter your commitment and relationship to the organization. Maintain enough detachment to know when it is time to move on and maintain enough courage to make the first step on your own behalf towards moving on.

Be Open To New Opportunities

Sometimes nothing is wrong with the current job and your sense of life purpose has not shifted, but an opportunity comes along that is fabulous. Those opportunities tend to come only to those who are open to them. If you cannot envision leaving what you perceive as the security of the current creative engagement, then you will be closed to those fabulous opportunities.

It is akin to a man who, upon inheriting a house, goes to examine his inheritance. He steps through the front door, sees a table before him, and notices a number of gold coins on the table. In this moment, he decides to make his home in this one room. He moves in. He spends his days in that one room, eats in that room, entertains in that room, and sleeps in that room. At the far end of the room, opposite the front door, is another door. He never opens it, never explores what is behind it and, so, never discovers that he lives with a handful of gold coins when the room beyond is filled with treasure, which is also his inheritance.

Leave the door open just enough to see the possibilities of treasure beyond it.

Periodically Consider The Grail Question

Shamanism exists within many traditions throughout the world. In the Celtic tradition, Arthurian legend can be enlightening when viewed from a shamanic perspective. Within Arthurian legend exists the wonderful stories of the Grail and within these stories lies one particular story concerning the Grail question. The Grail question may be one of the most important questions for you to ask yourself periodically throughout your career. *Whom does the Grail serve?*

Perceval has grown up in a forest, reared solely by his mother. Some say that his father and brothers were killed and his mother wanted to protect him from the evils of war and its attendant killing and death. One of her teachings is to ask many questions in life.

Perceval aspires to become a knight after encountering one or more of King Arthur's knights. Some say that the knights Perceval encountered bedazzled him so greatly that he thought them to be angels, subsequently following them to Camelot and the Round Table. Perceval does, indeed, become a knight. He has many adventures and, during one of them, is

---

given a piece of advice by an older knight named Governal who serves, for a time, as a kind of father figure and mentor. That piece of advice is to never speak out of turn or ask foolish questions.

Perceval takes this advice to heart, despite the fact that it has contradicted his mother's teachings. As it happens, this piece of advice will have a profound effect on his life.

While attempting to return to home and mother, Perceval encounters an impassable stream. He sees a Fisherman and asks if there is a way to cross. The Fisherman tells him that he has a small boat, but that it is clearly not large enough to accommodate Perceval's horse. He suggests that Perceval spend the night at his own home and gives him instructions on how to find it.

Perceval follows the instructions and finds not a house, but a castle. Actually, there seems to be nothing there at first, and then a castle appears out of the mist. Once he enters the castle, he finds, to his surprise, the Fisherman. He is dressed in royal robes and reclines on a couch. This is no ordinary fisherman but, in fact, the Fisher King. The Fisher King reclines not out of mere weariness or laziness, but because he has a wound that will not heal.

As it happens, the act that wounded the Fisher King also laid waste the King's lands. The vast Wasteland can only be restored to vitality if the Fisher King is healed.

Strange events now happen. The Fisher King's niece brings a sword into the room and gives it to the Fisher King. He gives the sword to Perceval. A squire passes by with a lance, the point of which drips with blood. A beautiful damsel passes by carrying a fabulous gold cup (called in those times a grail) embedded with jewels. Another damsel passes by carrying a silver serving dish.

Well...different accounts of the story say slightly different things. One fact is constant. While Perceval wants to ask questions, he does not. Certainly, his mother's training would have allowed it, but he has adopted the advice of a fatherly knight. The most provocative question he wants to ask is *Whom does the grail serve?* He remains silent in the face of these wonders, recalling the knight's admonition to neither speak out of turn nor ask foolish questions.

Perceval eventually goes to bed, arises the next day, and leaves the castle only to find that it has disappeared once he has crossed the moat bridge (or, as some legends proclaim, awakens to find the castle gone and himself sleeping on stones). The countryside around him is barren. It is, indeed, a wasteland.

Soon Perceval happens upon a young woman (and in some of the tales, she is a very ugly young woman). They converse and she discovers that Perceval has been in the castle of the Fisher King. This is highly unusual because the castle seems to blink in and out of ordinary reality, seldom seen or visited by mortals. She asks what he experienced there and he tells her. She inquires as to whether or not he asked any questions about what he saw there, particularly the grail. He admits that he did not and he learns, as she spits out the information in anger, that if he had asked the question he most wanted to ask, the Fisher King would have been restored to health and the barren lands would have been restored to life and productivity.

If this news is not bad enough, the young woman informs him that his mother is dead. His hard journey to return home is for naught.

Perceval now sees a quest before him, that of searching again for the illusive Fisher King's castle so that he can ask the right question.

In the story of Perceval and the Fisher King, the ability and willingness to ask the right questions is crucial. It is no less crucial in your career. While there are many ways to view the story, I will suggest an interpretation suitable for the career person.

The Grail may be viewed as a symbol of abundance (not the least of which is financial abundance) and life force. In Celtic traditions, one of the forms that the Grail takes is the cauldron of plenty, which can provide enough food to feed entire communities. From a psychological perspective, a cauldron (or cup or chalice), because of its shape, is sometimes thought to be highly suggestive of feminine energy—the womb from which all good things are formed and emerge. For career purposes, I relate the Grail to the abundance sought after by you and the company by whom you are employed. The search for the Grail, then, becomes the search for that abundance.

Perceval found himself in the Fisher King's castle, with mysterious and fascinating things happening around him, including a beautiful maiden who passes within his sight carrying the jewel-embedded Grail. Perceval wants very much to ask whom the Grail serves, but does not. While his mother has taught him to ask questions, his mentor has taught him to avoid asking too many questions. Unfortunately, he listens to his mentor instead of his mother and does not ask the question that could have restored the Fisher King to health and made abundant the wasteland.

When contemplating this story, keep in mind that it is appropriate to ask yourself whom your personal quest for abundance serves and to ask your employer whom the organization's profits/success serves. If the latter is more than you can muster the strength to do, ask *yourself* whom the employer's profit/success serves. Whom does the Grail serve? If the personal answer is that it serves only your personal needs, desires and whims, realize that this answer will define you and your work. If the employer answer is that it serves only the investors, realize that this answer will define the employer and how the employer operates. Yes, it has become the norm to hear from employers that the organization serves the investors alone. There is a common, and I believe misguided, belief that this is the only answer consistent with corporate survival. Challenge that answer, at least in your own mind. Challenge yourself to step into a grander version of yourself when you answer that question for yourself.

Do not stop there. One of Perceval's principle problems was that he listened to his mentor's advice (do not ask too many questions) instead of his mother's teachings (ask many questions). If Grail equals feminine energy and feminine energy equals abundance (at least in *this* story), to whom should he have been listening?

Ask questions. Ask many questions. Ask them of yourself. In fact, ask most of them of yourself because those questions will probably inspire behavior—and individual behavior is the one thing that changes everything on planet Earth. The best group action begins with the seeds planted by individuals who have thought deeply. Ask questions of yourself.

Ask questions of and about the employer. Whom the employer serves will determine how you are treated as an employee. It will determine the level of integrity with which the employer conducts business.

Think further yet. It could be argued that Perceval performs the role of the Fool, the young innocent, and the Fisher King performs the role of the jaded (wounded) older adult (king). The young innocent can, it would seem, heal the jaded older adult and return the wasteland to abundance by learning from Perceval's mistake. In fact, the adult can heal himself (or herself) by returning to the role of the innocent. Listen to your mother. Ask questions.

By the way, in some quarters there is an answer to the Grail question. Whom does the Grail serve? **The Grail serves everyone.**

Realize That The Journey Never Ends
And You Are Always Living The Dream

While life sometimes feels like a series of journeys with periods of rest between them, I believe it is actually an ongoing journey that began before you stepped into human form and will continue after you leave that form. Take time, often, to step back and consider the journey. Is it fulfilling and is it fun? If it does not contain these two components, consider revising your plan.

In shamanic terms, we are all *already* living the dream. Whether yours is a pleasant one or a nightmare is up to you. If the dream you are dreaming is not pleasing to you, then choose again; dream a new dream.

My wish for you is that your journey be fruitful, purposeful and enjoyable.

AFTERWORD

I believe that the journey you take, the dream that you dream, is forever inextricably linked to a Universe of Oneness. This Oneness is filled with love, an endless supply of it, which circulates in an ongoing hoop. It is one thing to understand this at an intellectual level and quite another to consciously experience it at a visceral level. Because *everything* related to your career is already a part of this hoop of loving and because your conscious experience of it can, I believe, enhance the journey, I suggest the following experiment.

The Hoop of Loving
(Also Found On Accompanying CD)

1. Sit comfortably straight in a chair. Close your eyes. Feel the connection of your feet with the floor and, as you feel this connection, allow yourself to experience your connection with Mother Earth and the gentle groundedness she provides.

2. Sense the top of your head, your crown, opening gently. A stream of light, pure love, passes from the Universe through this opening and into your body. Notice the color of the light. Sense this light, this pure love, filling your body completely, permeating each cell.

3. Allow the light to spill from your body passing through your skin, stretching outwards in all directions.

4. Notice that your personal supply of love is not depleted because you have a constant stream of the light of love entering your body, flowing through you.

5. Now focus the love in your body, creating a laser beam of love to pass from some part of your being, perhaps a part of you that you have experienced love flowing from in the past, such as your heart area or your third eye. Direct this beam of pure love to someone in your life.

Notice the love reaching them, regardless of where they are in the world, and entering their being.

6. Your personal supply of love continues to be full and rich and you notice the light of love continuing to flow into you.

7. Now, again focus the love in your body. This time, send a laser-focused beam of love from *another* part of your body, one you have not consciously directed love from in the past—perhaps your hands, solar plexus, or lower back. Direct this beam of love to another person. Do you experience this transfer of love in the same way as you did the first time, or do you experience it in a different way as it passes through a different part of your body? Is it curious or a surprise to you to experience this transfer of love in a way you may not have previously considered? Notice the love reaching the person to whom you are directing it.

8. Again, notice that your personal supply of love is not depleted, as the pure light of love continues to pass through you.

9. Now, focus a beam of love and direct it to: an animal, a tree, a boulder, your house, or anything else. Experience your beam of love reaching its target and entering the beingness of it. Do you experience this transfer of love in the same way as before or is it different in any way?

10. Now, simply sense the love flowing into you, the light of love flowing into your body through the top of your head. Notice that this flow of love light seems to consist of particles. You may be surprised as you notice that some of these particles of love light are the very particles *you sent* in a focused laser beam of love to another person, animal or object. These particles have passed from you and into them and have been directed out from them into the Universe, some of them *finding their way back to you.*

11. Experience the pleasure of realizing that your own sense of love, sent out from you, has found its way back to you. In this way, **you are pure love, loving itself. You experience the hoop of loving!** Allow yourself to be filled with this experience, to enjoy it fully.

12. Gently return your consciousness to the ordinary world around you, taking the fulfillment of this knowing with you and realizing that you can return to this experience at any time.

ENDNOTES

[1] Specifically, the modalities of Reiki and ARCH

[2] While shamanism is a complex subject, on which many books have been written, I will define it as simply as possible here: a worldview and practices, ancient in origin, that acknowledge the existence of alternate realities and the human ability to enter them, and that uses entry into altered states of consciousness for purposes of gathering information and/or healing.

[3] By Universal Principles, I mean *meta*-principles, the overarching and underlying "way things work" of the Universe, as we humans can comprehend it.

[4] Chödrön, Pema, *When Things Fall Apart* (Boston, Shambala Publications, Inc., 1997).

[5] A smudge stick, or smudge bundle, is a bundle of dried herb sprigs, tied tightly with string. Sage and sweat grass are two of the most popular, and traditional, herbs used for smudging. The smudge stick is lit with a match, then the flame is extinguished (**not** with water, but typically by blowing the flame out, waving the stick to extinguish the flame, or allowing the flame to extinguish itself), creating smoke to curl from the bundle. Smudging, using the smoke from the smudge bundle, is practiced as a way to purify space and personal energy. As with any fire, caution should be taken in using a smudge stick.

[6] Shamanic drumming is a drumming technique designed to slow body processes and facilitate altered states of consciousness.

[7] Ziegler, Warren, *Ways of Enspiriting* (Denver, FIA International LLC, 1994)

BENEDICTION

As with all journeys, difficult or easy, it is in the passage that our spirit is tested. Along the way we ask for guidance, a light, or signposts to help us navigate the treacherous straits with a good wind at our back and calm seas before us.

We ask for courage, determination and faith like that of the mustard seed. And at the zenith of our accomplishment, be it great or small, we pause and give tribute to those that bent to give a hand and to that which is greater than us. Then with spirit renewed, we set foot to the path on a new journey.

Antonio Arguello
Lakewood, Colorado
July, 2002

THIS FRAGILE BODY

Note: A few words from Nick Zelinger's song, *This Fragile Body*, are quoted at the beginning of this book's *Introduction*. They are quoted in full here, with Mr. Zelinger's permission.

This Fragile Body
By Nick Zelinger

I am not this fragile body, I am not this wicked mind.
I am, more or less, the whisper of a word
That flows through space and time.

By the river's edge the water rushes by me.
It's so much like my life, the struggle and the strife.
Every ebb and flow reminds me of the journey
That cannot be described and will not be denied.
Its silence welcomes me with opened arms.
And I settle like a stone.

I am not this fragile body, I am not this wicked mind.
I am, more or less, the whisper of a word
That flows through space and time.

In this solitude a thought can break the silence.
The sound it makes is clear as it echoes in my ear.
Every breath I take returns me to the moment,
Where silence has its sound, and my breath is soft and round
And smooth and flowing as this endless stream.
I am sinking like a stone.

I am not this fragile body, I am not this wicked mind.
I am, more or less, the whisper of a word
That flows through space and time.

©2001 Saxxon Woods Music

RESOURCES

Dragonheart
Melanie I Mulhall
1093 E. 3rd Ave.
Broomfield, CO 80020
www.thedragonheart.com
mmulhall@earthlink.net
303-469-5780

Dragonheart provides a suite of services including the following:
- Career/Job Search/Executive Coaching
- Change/Transition Facilitation
- Management/Human Resource Consulting
- Psych-K™
- The Birkman Method®
- Reiki/ARCH
- Shamanism

Melanie Mulhall is also available for workshops, presentations, speaking engagements, book signings, and contract work for the print media.

BC Communications
Ron Grandia
145 Dillon Ave., Suite C
Campbell, CA 95008
rgrandia@bccommunications.com
408-376-4001

BC Communications is a full-service production and creative services company specializing in helping businesses of all sizes and types create effective and compelling media and messages. Ron and his associates focus on "thinking like the audience."

Ron Grandia is the voice of the guided images on the CD that accompanies this book.

Sundance Media Group
Douglas Spotted Eagle
Box 3
Stockton, UT 84071
info@sundancemediagroup.com
435-882-8494
435-882-8508 (FAX)

Sundance Media Group provides a wide array of services including:
- Consulting and training
- Streaming Audio/Video for Internet/Intranet Delivery
- DVD and VCD authoring
- Corporate messaging
- Repurposing of existing media
- Digital media storage
- Video for broadcast

Sundance Media Group has an award winning staff and a client list that includes HBO, Showtime, Disney, Sonic Foundry, National Enquirer, REAL Networks, and countless school districts, corporations, and other organizations.

Douglas Spotted Eagle has won many awards, including the Grammy and Telly. He is a master of the Native American flute with many CDs to his credit. Douglas not only mixed, edited and mastered the CD that accompanies this book, he authored and performed on its original sound tracks.

NZ Graphics
Nick Zelinger
1445 S. Quail Court
Lakewood, CO 80232
Znick4@qwest.net
303-985-4174

NZ Graphics specializes in quality design and production of printed materials such as: company logos, book covers and interiors, brochures, pocket folders, business cards, letterhead, posters, annual reports, and product packaging. The firm also provides web site design services.

Nick Zelinger provided cover and interior design and layout for this book.

In addition to heading up NZ Graphics, Nick Zelinger is a member of the musical group, Saxxon Woods. His song, *This Fragile Body*, from the Saxxon Woods CD, *The Quarter Moon of Knowing*, was quoted in this book. Visit the Saxxon Woods web site at www.saxxonwoods.com.

Isaac Hartsell
isaacdesigner@aol.com
303-771-4125

Isaac Hartsell has studied art throughout his life and is a graduate of the Art Institute of Colorado. He has also studied animation, comic book art and airbrush technique at the Inkspinners School of Cartooning and commercial art at Pikes Peak Community College. Isaacís work has included business promotion art, t-shirt design/art, ad campaigns, film storyboard, tattoo painting, book cover design/art, and art instruction.

Isaac produced the original cover art for Living The Dream. If you are interested in obtaining a poster of the cover art or commissioning original artwork, contact Isaac by phone or e-mail.

Warren Ziegler
www.enspiriting.com
FIA International LLC
1335 Locust St.
Denver, CO 80220-2830
303-399-1077

The Center for Human Spirit
www.centerforhumanspirit.org
9038 Meadow Hill Circle
Lone Tree, CO 80124-5430

Warren Ziegler is the author of *Ways of Enspiriting: Transformative Practices for the Twenty-First Century* (available through www.enspiriting.com) and *When Your Spirit Calls–In Search of Your Spiritual Archetype* (available through www.Xlibris.com). Information on ordering audio tapes and workbooks can be found at www.enspiriting.com as well as resources for and information about the Enspiriting work. Information about the work of the Center for Human Spirit may be found at www.centerforhumanspirit.org.

The suggestions on Deep Listening™ found in this book's chapter entitled *When The Destination Is Unclear* come directly from Warren's Enspiriting practices.

Sally Cheyne McDonald
sallymcd@concentric.net
303-377-8496

Sally Cheyne McDonald is an internationally respected astrologer employing both ancient and modern astrological techniques to chart the clientís life path, reveal information about the subconscious and spirit, and open the doors to self-realization. Her approach is a spirited combination of astrological coaching and counseling, infused with considerable intuitive guidance.

Ms. McDonald is a regular contributor to both print and online astrological publications such as *Astroworld*, reflecting her interest in political and business astrology.

Ms. McDonald, referred to in this bookís chapter entitled *When The Destination Is Unclear*, is the author's personal astrologer.

Index

J

K & L

M

N

O

P

ABOUT THE AUTHOR

After twenty years in the field of human resources, Melanie Mulhall left corporate America, became apprenticed to a shaman, and transformed her life. She has been assisting others in transforming *their* lives ever since, through her company, Dragonheart. Writer, career coach, shaman, corporate consultant, change facilitator - Melanie has been described as all of these. She describes herself as a *midwife of the human spirit.*

Melanie's holistic approach honors the needs and life path of each individual. She is certified to administer and interpret The Birkman Method® and has completed advanced training in Psych-K™. Melanie is also a Reiki Master and is trained in the energy healing modality, ARCH. Grounded in both traditional business methodologies and those oriented to Universal Principles, Melanie practices her belief that life is a participation sport requiring both the left and right brain, best enacted using all parts of the human four-fold nature: mind, body, spirit and emotions.

Melanie assists individuals, groups, and companies discern and live their dreams across the country. She is living her dream in Colorado.

Visit the author's web site at www.thedragonheart.com.

ABOUT THE VOICE

When not expertly guiding you through your career/life journey on the CD accompanying this book, Voiceover Artist Ron Grandia can be heard in commercials for car dealerships, as well as on voice mail systems, infomercials, and crime stopper TV shows. He is thankful for the opportunity to say something interesting and useful every once in a while.

Ron's passion for sound, in all its rich and varied forms, found voice during a ten-year stint as operator of a pirate, 40 watt radio station. This idyllic pass-time was, sadly, brought to a close when the FCC registered its disapproval, despite the enthusiastic approval of the pirate station's fans.

When not talking for a living, Ron operates BC Communications, a full-service production and creative service company specializing in helping companies of all sizes and types create effective, compelling media and messages. From concept and writing to final production, Ron and his associates focus on "thinking like the audience," so the customer doesn't have to.

Ron is living the dream with his family in San Jose, California.

A NOTE ABOUT THE CD

The CD that accompanies this book is comprised of some of the book's guided imageries and is intended to assist the reader in experiencing them optimally. When you reach a guided imagery designated as being on the accompanying CD, you may want to read through it, then put the book down, cue up the CD, sit back, and experience the imagery fully. Because each person's experience of any guided imagery is unique, you may find it helpful to pause the recording in places to allow yourself as much time as you need to have a rich and full experience.

You may also find benefit in experiencing these guided imageries a number of times, as new insights are possible with each listening.

Warning: Do not play this CD while driving a vehicle, operating equipment, or otherwise engaged in activity that could prove hazardous when done conjointly with listening to and experiencing the CD's content.